The Declarative Mind

Programming Without How

Fang Li, PhD

First Edition: November 2024

To my family,
who make everything possible

Give Thanks

This book would not have been possible without the unwavering support of my family. To my wife Jessica – thank you for being my foundation and inspiration. To our children Steven, Cleven, and Vivien – you fill my life with joy and purpose.

A special acknowledgment goes to Dr. Gopal Gupta, my PhD advisor, who introduced me to the elegant world of declarative programming. Your mentorship has not only shaped my academic journey but has led me to write this book to share this knowledge with others.

I am deeply grateful to all my students whose curiosity, questions, and enthusiasm have been a constant source of inspiration. Your eagerness to learn and understand declarative programming has motivated me to create this book and make these concepts more accessible to others.

Finally, I want to express my gratitude to all the friends, colleagues, and mentors who have supported and encouraged me along this journey. Your presence, conversations, and support have enriched both this book and my life in countless ways.

Preface

In the world of programming, there's a peculiar phenomenon I've observed over my years as a computer science professor: most programmers are trapped in a single way of thinking. They write code by meticulously telling the computer how to perform each step, a style known as imperative programming. It's like giving driving directions by listing every turn and street name, rather than simply showing a map and saying "get me to the airport."

There's another way – declarative programming. Instead of specifying how to do something, you declare what you want to achieve. It's a profound shift in thinking that transforms programming from giving instructions to expressing intentions. This book is my attempt to open this door for you, to show you that programming can be more about describing your problem than detailing its solution.

The timing of this book is particularly relevant. With the rise of large language models like ChatGPT, we're witnessing a fascinating shift in how humans interact with computers. When people use these AI systems, they're inadvertently practicing declarative thinking: they describe what they want ("write a business proposal", "analyze this data", "explain this concept") rather than how to do it. This emerging practice has been dubbed "prompt engineering", though as a computer scientist, I find this term somewhat lacking in academic rigor.

In the AI research community, we have a more formal concept called "knowledge engineering" – a systematic approach to representing and reasoning about knowledge. While there's currently a gap between this theoretical framework and the practical use of generative AI, I believe the future of AI will be fundamentally declarative. We're moving toward a world where we'll express our intentions to computers in increasingly natural ways, and they'll figure out how to achieve our goals.

This pocket-sized book introduces three main paradigms of declarative programming: functional programming, logic programming, and Answer Set Programming (ASP). It's not meant to be a comprehensive tutorial or textbook. Rather, think of it as a guided tour through these fascinating landscapes. My goal isn't to make you an expert in Haskell, Prolog, or ASP solvers, but to show you that there are different ways to think about programming – ways that might be more natural for certain problems.

As we explore these paradigms, you'll see how they relate to modern challenges in AI and software development. You'll understand why declarative approaches are often more elegant and maintainable than their imperative counterparts. Most importantly, you'll gain a new perspective on what it means to program a computer.

The future of computing is not about telling machines how

to do things – it's about expressing what we want to achieve and letting machines figure out the how. This shift is already happening in AI, and understanding declarative programming will help you be better prepared for this future.

Whether you are a seasoned programmer comfortable with imperative languages, a student exploring different programming paradigms, or someone interested in the future of AI and computing, I hope this book will expand your horizons and show you new ways of thinking about problem-solving.

Let's begin this journey into the world of declarative programming, where we focus on what we want to achieve rather than how to achieve it.

Fang Li

Nov, 2024

Contents

Shifting Your Mind (Introduction)

We've Been Programming Wrong?

The Recipe Paradox

Imagine you're hungry for a perfect chocolate cake. You have two magical kitchens at your disposal, and two very different ways to get your cake.

In Kitchen A, you must provide a detailed, step-by-step recipe: "Preheat oven to 350°F. Take out a clean bowl. Measure exactly 2 cups of flour. Sift the flour three times. Crack three eggs, one by one, checking each for shell fragments. Beat eggs for precisely 2 minutes at medium speed..."

The instructions go on and on, specifying every minute detail – the exact angle to hold the spatula, the precise number of times to stir, the exact seconds to wait between steps. Miss a single detail, and your cake might fail. Change your oven brand? You'll need to rewrite parts of the recipe. Want to make a bigger cake? You'll have to recalculate every measurement and timing.

Now, step into Kitchen B. Here, something remarkable happens. You simply declare: "I want a moist chocolate cake, three layers, with dark chocolate ganache frosting, serving 12 people. It should be rich but not too sweet, with a hint of espresso."

In this kitchen, those few descriptive words are enough. The kitchen understands cakes – their chemistry, the interactions between ingredients, the optimal techniques. It knows how to adjust for your altitude, humidity, and available ingredients. It knows how to scale the recipe up or down. Most importantly, it knows all the "how" so you don't have to.

Kitchen A is like traditional, imperative programming – specifying every single step, managing every detail, accounting for every possible scenario. It's exhausting, error-prone, and inflexible.

Kitchen B represents declarative programming. You focus on what you want, not how to get it. You describe the destination, not the journey. The system handles the complexity, drawing upon its deep understanding of the problem domain.

"But that's impossible!" you might say. "Computers need to be told exactly what to do!"

Do they really? When you use Google Maps, do you specify every turn, or do you simply enter your destination? When you use SQL to query a database, do you tell it how to search through the tables, or do you just describe the data you want?

What if we could program everything this way? What if we could solve complex problems by simply describing what we want, leaving the "how" to powerful solving engines? What if we could free our minds from the tyranny of step-by-step instructions and focus on the essence of what we're trying to achieve?

This is not just a dream. This is declarative programming, and it's already changing how we solve problems in the digital age. Welcome to a new way of thinking about programming – one where we focus on what, not how.

What, not How?

As we step back from our tale of two kitchens, a fundamental question emerges: can we really abstract away the complexities of programming as easily as our magical Kitchen B suggests? This section explores why this question strikes at the heart of how we've traditionally approached software development, and why rethinking our approach could revolutionize how we create software.

You might be thinking, "Sure, a magical kitchen sounds wonderful, but real programming can't be that simple." After all, we've spent decades telling computers exactly what to do, step by step. We've built entire industries around detailed instructions and precise procedures. We've trained generations of programmers to think in terms of "how."

But this obsession with "how" comes at a cost – a burden that grows heavier as our software systems become more complex. Just as our recipe in Kitchen A became unwieldy with its detailed instructions, traditional programming often drowns us in a sea of implementation details.

Let's examine this burden more closely. Imagine you're a software developer maintaining a large codebase. Like a chef trying to modify a thousand-step recipe, you find yourself wrestling with questions like:

"What happens if I change this line of code?" "How will this affect other parts of the system?" "What if the underlying hardware changes?" "How do I scale this solution?"

Every "how" adds another layer of complexity, another potential point of failure, another detail to maintain. Consider a simple task like sorting a list of numbers. In traditional programming, you might write:

```
for i in range(len(numbers)):
    for j in range(len(numbers) - 1):
        if numbers[j] > numbers[j + 1]:
            numbers[j], numbers[j + 1] = numbers[j +
                1], numbers[j]
```

But in declarative programming, you simply express:

```
sorted_numbers = sort(numbers)
```

The difference is striking. In the first approach, you're burdened with implementation details – loop counters, comparisons, swap operations. In the second, you simply declare what you want: a sorted list.

The weight of these implementation details isn't just a theoretical concern – it's a daily struggle that impacts everything from code maintenance to innovation speed. As we'll explore in the next section, "The Burden of 'How' in Traditional Programming," these challenges manifest in specific, costly ways that affect developers and organizations alike. By examining these concrete examples, we'll better understand why a fundamental shift in our approach isn't just desirable – it's becoming increasingly necessary in our complex, rapidly evolving technological landscape.

The Burden of "How" in Traditional Programming

Imagine you're building a house. In the imperative world, you'd need to describe every single movement of every construction worker: "Lift your right foot 8 inches, move it forward 12 inches, place it down. Pick up brick number 437 with your left hand..." Absurd, isn't it? Yet this is exactly how we write imperative programs.

Let's look at three everyday programming tasks that demonstrate this burden:

The String Processing Predicament

Consider extracting all unique email addresses from a text document. Here's what it looks like in traditional imperative style:

```python
def extract_emails(text):
    emails = set()
    words = text.split()
    for word in words:
        word = word.strip('.,!?()[]{}')
        if '@' in word:
            if word.count('@') == 1:
                local, domain = word.split('@')
                if '.' in domain:
                    if local and domain:
                        emails.add(word.lower())
    return list(emails)
```

```
text = "Contact john.doe@example.com or
    SUPPORT@company.com for help!"
email_list = extract_emails(text)
```

Now, the declarative way using a regular expression:

```
import re

text = "Contact john.doe@example.com or
    SUPPORT@company.com for help!"
email_list = list(set(re.findall(r'\b[\w\.-]+@[\w
    \.-]+\.\w+\b', text.lower())))
```

The imperative version forces you to think about string splitting, character checking, nested conditions, and maintaining a set for uniqueness. The declarative version simply says "find all patterns that look like email addresses." Which would you rather debug?

The Database Dilemma

Imagine finding all employees who earned more than $50,000 in 2023. Here's the imperative approach:

```
employees = []
for record in database:
    if record.year == 2023:
        if record.salary > 50000:
            employee = get_employee_details(record.id)
            employees.append(employee)
```

```
for employee in employees:
    print(f"{employee.name}: ${employee.salary}")
```

Now, the SQL (declarative) way:

```
SELECT name, salary
FROM employees
WHERE salary > 50000 AND year = 2023;
```

The imperative approach forces you to manage iteration, filtering, and data collection. The declarative approach simply states what you want.

The Layout Labyrinth

Consider centering a div on a webpage. The old imperative way:

```
const div = document.getElementById('myDiv');
const windowHeight = window.innerHeight;
const windowWidth = window.innerWidth;
const divHeight = div.offsetHeight;
const divWidth = div.offsetWidth;

div.style.position = 'absolute';
div.style.top = (windowHeight - divHeight) / 2 + 'px';
div.style.left = (windowWidth - divWidth) / 2 + 'px';

window.addEventListener('resize', function() {
    const windowHeight = window.innerHeight;
    const windowWidth = window.innerWidth;
    div.style.top = (windowHeight - divHeight) / 2 + '
      px';
```

```
      div.style.left = (windowWidth - divWidth) / 2 + '
          px';
});
```

The declarative CSS way:

```
.centered-div {
    display: flex;
    justify-content: center;
    align-items: center;
    height: 100vh;
}
```

The imperative approach requires manual calculation of positions, explicit handling of window resizing, and managing multiple style properties. In contrast, the declarative approach simply describes the desired layout: "center this content both vertically and horizontally." The browser handles all the complex calculations and updates automatically.

The Maintenance Nightmare

These examples reveal a darker truth: the burden of "how" doesn't end with initial implementation. Every step-by-step instruction becomes a potential point of failure, a maintenance liability:

- What if the requirements change slightly?

- What if we need to optimize for different conditions?

- What if we need to debug an issue?

• What if new team members need to understand the code?

In the imperative world, each of these questions often leads to hours of code archaeology, trying to understand not just what the code does, but how it does it. Each modification risks breaking the careful choreography of steps.

The cognitive load is immense. Your brain must simultaneously track:

• Loop variables and their scope

• State changes and their timing

• Edge cases and boundary conditions

• Performance implications

• Error handling at each step

It's like trying to juggle while reciting Shakespeare – you're managing so many details that you lose sight of the actual goal.

The weight of imperative programming isn't just about writing code – it's about carrying that code forward through time. Each step-by-step instruction we write today becomes tomorrow's technical debt. It's like leaving detailed instructions for every possible scenario to future inhabitants of a house: "If the light bulb burns out on a rainy Tuesday during winter, then..."

The real cost isn't in the initial writing – it's in the ongoing cognitive overhead. Every time we revisit code, we must mentally execute each step, understand each decision point, and carefully consider the ripple effects of any changes. This mental taxation pulls us away from solving real problems and innovating.

But perhaps the greatest irony is that computers don't actually need these detailed instructions. Modern hardware and software systems are incredibly sophisticated – they're capable of finding optimal solutions if we just tell them what we want. By insisting on specifying every detail, we're not just burdening ourselves; we're often preventing the computer from finding better solutions.

New Hope?

If the burden of "how" is so heavy, what's the alternative? This is where the power of "what" comes into play. Imagine if we could program like we think – in terms of goals and outcomes rather than steps and procedures. Instead of writing detailed instructions for solving problems, what if we could simply describe our problems clearly?

This isn't just a programmer's fantasy. In fact, you're already using this approach in many aspects of your digital life, perhaps without realizing it. When you use a smart speaker, you don't give it step-by-step instructions for playing music – you just tell it what you want to hear. When you use modern AI tools, you describe what you want rather than how to create it.

In the next section, we'll explore how this same principle – the power of describing "what" instead of "how" – can transform the way we approach programming. We'll see how this shift in thinking not only lightens our cognitive load but often leads to more robust, maintainable, and efficient solutions.

Introduction to Thinking Declaratively

The shift to declarative thinking begins with a simple yet profound question: "What if we could just describe our problems instead of their solutions?"

Think of yourself as an architect rather than a construction worker. An architect doesn't specify the exact muscle movements for laying each brick; they create blueprints that describe what they want to build. This is declarative thinking in action.

The Mental Shift

Moving to declarative thinking requires a fundamental transformation in how we approach problems. This shift happens across three crucial dimensions, each representing a departure from traditional programming habits.

First, we must transition from "How" to "What." This means breaking free from our instinct to immediately jump into step-by-step solutions. Instead of writing code that says "first do this, then do that," we learn to step back and clearly articulate our desired outcome. It's like the difference between giving someone turn-by-turn directions and simply showing them a picture of the destination. When we focus on describing problems clearly, we often discover that the solution becomes more apparent, and sometimes, we realize we were solving the wrong problem altogether.

The second shift moves us from Control to Declaration. This

is perhaps the most challenging transition for experienced programmers because it requires us to let go. We've been trained to account for every edge case, to handle every possible scenario, to control every aspect of execution. But declarative thinking asks us to trust in specialized solving engines that often understand their domains better than we do. Modern database engines, for instance, can optimize queries far better than most hand-coded solutions. By embracing higher-level abstractions, we gain access to sophisticated solutions that adapt to changing conditions automatically.

The third transformation involves moving from State Management to State Description. Traditional programming often feels like juggling – keeping track of multiple changing variables, managing transitions, and handling edge cases. Declarative thinking flips this model. Instead of tracking how things change over time, we focus on describing valid states and the rules for transformation. We define what constitutes a valid state and let the system worry about maintaining consistency. Think of it like describing the rules of chess rather than writing code for every possible move sequence.

This mental metamorphosis yields remarkable benefits. Solutions become more robust because they're built on well-defined states and transformations rather than brittle step-by-step procedures. Scalability improves naturally because declarative systems can often parallelize operations and optimize execution paths without explicit instructions. Maintenance becomes easier since we're working with higher-level concepts rather than low-level details. Code intent becomes clearer because we're expressing what we want rather than how to get it. And perhaps most importantly, problem-solving becomes more efficient because we're operating at the level of the problem domain rather than the implementation details.

Consider a database query optimizer. When we write declarative SQL, we're not just saving ourselves from writing complex iteration logic – we're allowing the database engine to adapt our query to changing data patterns, server conditions, and available resources. The same query might execute differently as the data grows or as usage patterns change, all without requiring modifications to our code.

This shift in thinking does more than change how we write code – it changes how we solve problems. It elevates us from the role of instruction-writers to problem-describers, from micromanagers to architects. In doing so, it frees both us and our computers to do what each does best: humans focusing on what needs to be accomplished, and computers determining how best to accomplish it.

Core Principles of Declarative Thinking

These principles form a cohesive framework for approaching problems declaratively. Each builds upon the previous one, creating a comprehensive approach to problem-solving.

1. **Separation of Intent and Implementation**

   The foundation of declarative thinking is separating what we want to achieve from how it's achieved. This principle encourages us to express our goals clearly without getting lost in implementation details.

Instead of writing:

```python
def find_user(users, target_id):
    for user in users:
        if user.id == target_id:
            return user
    return None
```

You express your intent:

```python
user = users.find(id: target_id)
```

2. **Focus on Relationships and Constraints**

Rather than writing procedures to enforce rules, we define the relationships and constraints that must hold true. This approach makes our intentions clearer and allows systems to optimize enforcement.

Imperative Thinking:

```python
def validate_order(order):
    if order.total < 0:
        return False
    if order.items.length == 0:
        return False
    if order.delivery_date < today:
        return False
    return True
```

Declarative Thinking:

```sql
CONSTRAINT valid_order CHECK (
    total >= 0 AND
```

```
    items_count > 0 AND
    delivery_date >= CURRENT_DATE
)
```

3. **Describing States, Not Steps**

   Instead of manually managing transitions between states, we declare the desired states and let the system handle the transitions. This principle significantly reduces complexity in state management.

   Instead of writing:

```
function toggleMenu() {
    const menu = document.getElementById('menu');
    if (menu.style.display === 'none') {
        menu.style.display = 'block';
        menu.style.opacity = '0';
        setTimeout(() => {
            menu.style.opacity = '1';
        }, 10);
    } else {
        menu.style.opacity = '0';
        setTimeout(() => {
            menu.style.display = 'none';
        }, 300);
    }
}
```

Describe desired states:

```
.menu {
    transition: opacity 0.3s;
}
.menu.visible {
```

```
        opacity: 1;
        display: block;
}
```

4. **Embracing Immutability**

   Immutability is a powerful concept in declarative programming. Instead of modifying data in place, we describe transformations that produce new data. This makes our code easier to reason about and often more maintainable.

   Imperative way:

```
def process_data(data):
    for i in range(len(data)):
        data[i] = data[i] * 2
        if data[i] > 10:
            data[i] = 10
```

   Describe transformations:

```
processed_data = data.map(lambda x: min(x * 2,
    10))
```

5. **Thinking in Patterns**

   The final principle involves recognizing and leveraging common patterns. Instead of writing custom logic for common operations, we use established patterns that clearly communicate intent.

   Procedural patterns:

```
total = 0
for item in items:
```

```
if item.category == "electronics":
        total += item.price
```

Declarative patterns:

```
total = items.filter(category="electronics").sum(
    price)
```

While this mental shift might seem abstract, you're already thinking declaratively in many aspects of your daily life – often without realizing it. The same way you don't tell your coffee maker which circuits to energize or how to control its heating element (you just press "brew"), you're constantly interacting with the world through declarations of intent rather than detailed instructions.

These natural examples can serve as powerful mental models for understanding declarative programming. Just as the GPS revolution freed us from memorizing routes and watching for street signs, declarative programming can liberate us from the burden of specifying computational details. By examining these everyday analogies, we can build an intuitive understanding of declarative thinking that extends far beyond code.

Let's explore some familiar scenarios where we've already made the shift from "how" to "what" in our daily lives, and see how these parallel our journey in programming. These examples will show us that declarative thinking isn't just a programming paradigm – it's a natural evolution in how humans interact with increasingly sophisticated systems.

Real-world Analogies of Declarative Thinking

The modern world is filled with examples where we've naturally evolved from procedural to declarative approaches. These everyday transitions mirror the evolution we're seeing in programming and offer valuable insights into the power of declarative thinking.

Photography: From Darkroom to Instagram

Remember manual photography? Every photo required precise calculations:

```
1. Measure light levels with a meter
2. Calculate the exposure triangle (aperture, shutter
   speed, ISO)
3. Adjust focus manually
4. Process film with exact chemical ratios and timing
5. Print photos with careful exposure control
```

Today, we simply say:

```
"Take a portrait with blurred background"
"Make this photo more vibrant"
"Adjust this to look like sunset"
```

Modern computational photography handles thousands of calculations automatically, often producing better results than manual settings ever could. The camera understands photographic principles so well that we can focus on what we want to capture rather than how to capture it.

Navigation: From Maps to Modern GPS

The evolution of navigation perfectly illustrates the power of declarative thinking:

Traditional Navigation (Imperative):

```
1. Find current location on map
2. Identify optimal route considering:
   - Road types
   - Traffic patterns
   - Distance vs. time
3. Memorize sequence of turns
4. Monitor street signs
5. Recalculate if you miss a turn
```

Modern Navigation (Declarative):

```
"Take me to the airport, avoiding highways"
```

The GPS system manages countless variables we never see:

- Real-time traffic conditions

- Road closures and construction

- Optimal route recalculation

- Alternative routes when needed

- Elevation and road type considerations

Smart Home Automation: From Timers to Intentions

Consider how we manage our living spaces:

Traditional Home Management (Imperative):

```
1. Set timer for lights at 7pm
2. Adjust thermostat before bed
3. Check if doors are locked
4. Turn off unused appliances
5. Open blinds in morning
```

Modern Smart Home (Declarative):

```
home_rules:
    - "Keep the house comfortable when we're home"
    - "Secure the house when we leave"
    - "Save energy when possible"
```

The system handles complex interactions:

- Learns occupancy patterns

- Adjusts for seasonal changes

- Balances comfort and energy efficiency

- Coordinates multiple devices

- Adapts to unexpected events

Music and Entertainment: From Mix Tapes to Streaming

Remember creating the perfect playlist?

Traditional Music Collection (Imperative):

```
1. Buy albums
2. Select specific songs
3. Arrange in perfect order
4. Record onto cassette
5. Create backup copies
```

Modern Streaming (Declarative):

```
"Play something I'll like"
"Create a workout mix"
"Set the mood for dinner"
```

The streaming service:

- Analyzes music patterns

- Understands personal preferences

- Adapts to current context

- Discovers relevant new content

- Maintains flow and variety

Cooking: From Precise Recipes to Smart Appliances

Even cooking has evolved:

Traditional Cooking (Imperative):

```
1. Preheat to exactly 350 F
2. Stir every 2 minutes
3. Cook for exactly 12 minutes
4. Rest for 5 minutes
```

Modern Smart Cooking (Declarative):

```
"Cook rice"
"Prepare medium-rare steak"
"Keep food warm until dinner"
```

Smart appliances now:

- Adjust cooking parameters automatically

- Monitor food doneness

- Compensate for variations

- Maintain optimal conditions

- Ensure consistent results

The Common Thread

These real-world transitions reveal three fundamental principles of declarative systems:

Intent-Driven Interaction Users communicate goals rather than procedures, allowing systems to leverage their sophisticated understanding of the domain.

Adaptive Intelligence Systems continuously learn and optimize, often achieving better results than manual approaches could provide.

Complexity Management The underlying complexity is handled automatically, presenting users with simple, intuitive interfaces while maintaining robust error handling.

These patterns in everyday technology preview the future of programming itself. As we'll see in the next section, modern programming frameworks and languages are evolving along similar lines, enabling developers to work at higher levels of abstraction while achieving better results.

Declarative Programming: Three Paths to Freedom

Remember when we talked about focusing on "what" instead of "how"? Well, smart people have actually created entire programming paradigms around this idea. Think of them as three different languages that all speak the truth of declarative thinking, just with different accents.

The Family Portrait

Imagine you're trying to explain your family structure to someone. You could do it by walking them through a step-by-step process of how to trace relationships ("first go to my mom, then look at her sister, then..."). Or you could simply state the relationships that exist: "Alice is my aunt, and she's my mom's sister." That's the essence of what these three paradigms do – they let us state truths rather than procedures.

These three paradigms – functional, logic, and answer set programming – are like siblings in a family. They share the same declarative DNA, but each has developed their own unique personality and strengths. Think of them as three different artists painting the same landscape: one might use watercolors, another oils, and the third charcoal, but they're all capturing the same scene.

Functional programming is like the methodical sibling who loves organizing things and keeping everything in its proper place. Give them a messy room, and they'll transform it into a perfectly ordered space – not by giving you a detailed cleaning manual, but by defining what "clean" means and making sure everything fits that definition.

Logic programming is the detective in the family, always asking "why" and making connections. They don't solve mysteries by following a predetermined script, but by understanding relationships and letting conclusions naturally emerge from known facts.

Answer set programming is the puzzle enthusiast, who can look at a complex set of constraints and somehow find solutions that make everyone happy. They don't need to know how to search for solutions – they just need to know what makes a solution valid.

What makes this family special is how they complement each other. While they might approach problems differently, they all share the same fundamental belief: that programming should be about describing the problem space rather than prescribing exact solutions. It's like the difference between telling someone "get me a drink that's refreshing, caffeinated, and not too sweet" versus giving them step-by-step instructions for making a specific beverage.

In the world of traditional, imperative programming, we've been writing detailed instruction manuals. With declarative programming, we're writing specifications instead. The computer becomes our partner in problem-solving rather than just a blind executor of instructions. This shift in perspective is what makes declarative programming so powerful – and sometimes so challenging for developers trained in traditional approaches.

As we explore each member of this family in the coming chapters, you'll see how their individual strengths can be applied to different types of problems. More importantly, you'll learn how their shared declarative nature can fundamentally change the way you think about problem-solving in programming.

Functional Programming: Transforming Data

Let's start with perhaps the most approachable one. Functional programming is like having a really efficient assembly line for your data. Instead of telling the computer "take this number, put it in a loop, increment the counter, multiply each time...", you simply say "I want all these numbers doubled."

Instead of:

```
for (i = 0; i < list.length; i++) {
    result[i] = list[i] * 2;
}
```

You write:

```
map(double, [1,2,3])
```

It's like the difference between giving someone detailed instructions to make a sandwich versus saying "I want a BLT." The what, not the how. This is just scratching the surface – in the Functional Mind chapter, we'll explore how this approach leads to code that's not just cleaner, but also more reliable and easier to reason about. We'll see how concepts like immutability and pure functions transform the way we think about program design.

Logic Programming: Describing Relationships

Now, imagine you're a detective solving a mystery. Instead of writing out every possible step to solve it, what if you could just describe the clues and relationships you know, and let the computer figure out the solution? That's logic programming.

Instead of writing complex if-then-else chains, you can do this way:

```
parent(john, mary).
parent(mary, bob).
grandparent(X, Z) :- parent(X, Y), parent(Y, Z).
```

You're essentially creating a mini universe of facts and rules, then asking questions about it. It's like writing a mystery novel where you describe all the characters and their relationships, then letting the reader figure out who did it. When we get to the Logical Mind chapter, you'll discover how this approach can handle complex reasoning tasks with surprising elegance, and how it's being used in everything from medical diagnosis to natural language processing.

Answer Set Programming: Declaring Constraints and Common Sense

Here's where things get really interesting. Sometimes, you don't want to transform data or query relationships – you want to find a solution that satisfies a bunch of rules, including rules about what's not true. Think about planning a party: "Alice can't sit next to Bob, everyone needs to sit next to at least one friend, and we need equal numbers on each side of the table."

Instead of writing complex scheduling algorithms, you can do this:

```
1 {seat(Person, Position) : Position(1..6)} 1 :-
    person(Person).
:- seat(alice, P1), seat(bob, P2), |P1-P2| = 1.
:- not balanced_sides.
```

Look at how naturally this reads – the first line says each person needs exactly one seat (that's what the 1 ... 1 means). The second line is a constraint saying Alice and Bob can't sit in adjacent positions. The third line enforces that the sides must be balanced. We're not telling the computer how to search for a valid seating arrangement – we're just stating what makes an arrangement valid. The ASP solver figures out the "how" for us.

But ASP goes even further. It can handle something that's surprisingly hard in traditional programming: common-sense reasoning. Imagine you're booking a restaurant. If the menu doesn't mention vegan options, you'd probably assume there aren't any. This kind of "reasoning about what's not there" is natural for humans but tricky for computers. ASP handles this elegantly through what's called "negation as failure" – if it can't prove something is true, it assumes it's false, just like we often do in daily life.

```
has_vegan_options(R) :- restaurant(R),
    explicitly_vegan(R).
```

```
not_suitable_for_vegans(R) :- restaurant(R), not
    has_vegan_options(R).
```

This might seem like a small detail, but it's actually a super-power – it lets ASP revise its conclusions when new information arrives, just like humans do. We'll dive deep into this fascinating capability in the Answer Set Programming chapter, where you'll see how this makes ASP particularly good at handling real-world scenarios where information is incomplete or changing.

You just state the rules and what you assume in the absence of information, and the system figures out all possible solutions that make sense. No need to write code for how to find these arrangements or handle all the special cases.

Buckle Up, the Journey Starts!

We've come a long way in this chapter – from recognizing the burden of "how" in our traditional programming approaches, through understanding what declarative thinking really means, to seeing it reflected in our daily lives and modern technologies. We've also gotten our first glimpse of the three powerful paradigms that make declarative programming possible: functional programming with its elegant data transformations, logic programming with its intelligent relationship reasoning, and answer set programming with its constraint-based problem solving. Now that we understand the "why" of declarative programming and have seen its reflections in the world around us, it's time to dive deeper into how these paradigms work in practice. Let's start our journey with functional programming – perhaps the most widely adopted of the three approaches. In the next chapter, "The Functional Mind," we'll discover how thinking in transformations rather than steps can revolutionize the way we solve problems, and how the principles of immutability and pure functions can lead to code that's not just more elegant, but more reliable and maintainable. Ready to see how functions can be so much more than just procedures?

The Functional Mind

Remember when you first learned programming? You probably started with something like "First do this, then do that, then if this happens, do something else..." It's how most of us were taught to think about programming – as a series of steps, like a recipe. But what if I told you that some of the most elegant solutions in programming come from thinking about what things are rather than what steps to take?

More than Procedures

Let's start with a story. A junior developer, Sarah, was tasked with processing a large dataset of customer transactions. Her first instinct was to write code the way she always had:

```python
def process_transactions(transactions):
    results = []
    for t in transactions:
        if t.status == 'completed':
            amount = t.amount
            if t.currency != 'USD':
                amount = convert_to_usd(amount, t.
                    currency)
            if amount > 1000:
                amount = apply_large_transaction_fee(
                    amount)
            processed = {
                'id': t.id,
                'final_amount': amount,
                'processed_date': datetime.now()
            }
            results.append(processed)
    return results
```

Looking at this code, her tech lead asked her a simple question: "What is this function actually doing?" Sarah started explaining the steps: "Well, first it loops through the transactions, then it checks if each one is completed, then it converts the currency if needed..."

"No," her lead interrupted, "I meant what is this function?

Not how does it do it."

After a moment of thought, Sarah replied: "It's... taking completed transactions and converting them to standardized USD records with fees applied?"

"Exactly! So why don't we write it that way?"

For our examples, we'll be using **Haskell**, one of the most popular purely functional programming languages. Don't worry if you've never seen Haskell before – we'll explain the syntax as we go. Haskell was chosen because it embodies the functional thinking principles we're learning about, and it makes it nearly impossible to fall back into procedural habits. It's like learning a new language by immersing yourself in a country where nobody speaks your native tongue – you're forced to think in the new way. While you don't need to become a Haskell expert, seeing these examples in a purely functional language will help cement these new thought patterns.

```
processTransactions :: [Transaction] -> [
    ProcessedTransaction]
processTransactions =
    filter isCompleted
    >>> map standardizeToUSD
    >>> map applyFeesIfNeeded
    >>> map addProcessingMetadata
```

Don't worry if this syntax looks alien – let's break it down. In Haskell, >>> is like a pipeline operator that says "take the result of this and feed it into the next function." It's similar to how we might chain methods in other languages. The map function applies a transformation to each item in a list – think of it as a more elegant version of a for-loop.

If we wrote this in a more familiar Python style using method chaining, it might look something like this:

```
def process_transactions(transactions):
    return (transactions
            .filter(is_completed)
            .map(standardize_to_usd)
            .map(apply_fees_if_needed)
            .map(add_processing_metadata))
```

This was Sarah's first glimpse into functional thinking. The new version wasn't just shorter – it was clearer about its purpose. Each line described a transformation of the data, not a set of instructions. The function became a pipeline of what needed to happen, not how to make it happen.

But the real beauty emerged when requirements changed. The business now wanted to process transactions in batches, apply different fee structures, and generate audit logs. In the original version, these changes would mean diving into the middle of that nested logic, carefully adjusting conditions and adding new steps. In the functional version? Each new requirement simply became a new transformation in the pipeline.

```
processTransactions :: [Transaction] -> ([
    ProcessedTransaction], AuditLog)
processTransactions =
    groupIntoBatches
    >>> map (filter isCompleted)
    >>> map (map standardizeToUSD)
    >>> map (map applyFeesWithNewStructure)
    >>> map (map addProcessingMetadata)
```

```
>>> generateAuditLog
```

Here, we have nested map operations because we're working with batches of transactions – essentially, lists of lists. Each outer map applies an operation to each batch, and each inner map applies an operation to each transaction within a batch.

Don't worry if you don't grasp all the Haskell syntax right away – the key is to understand that we're describing a series of transformations our data goes through, rather than the step-by-step instructions for how to process it. As we progress through this chapter, we'll introduce Haskell concepts gradually, always focusing on the thinking pattern rather than the syntax details.

This isn't just about making code shorter or even clearer – it's about thinking differently about what functions are. In traditional programming, we think of functions as procedures – series of steps to follow. In functional programming, we think of them as transformations – descriptions of how one thing becomes another.

Think about a coffee machine. The procedural way would be: "Add water, heat to 200°F, add grounds, wait 3 minutes, filter..." The functional way? "It's a transformation from water and coffee beans into coffee." Both describe the same thing, but one focuses on how, while the other focuses on what.

This shift in thinking – from procedures to transformations – is your first step into the functional mind. It's not just about learning new syntax or following different rules. It's about seeing programming problems in a new light, where solutions emerge from composing transformations rather than orchestrating steps.

And here's the thing: once you start thinking this way, you can't unsee it. You'll start noticing opportunities for transformations everywhere. That complex user interface logic? It's a transformation from application state to user interface elements. That data processing pipeline? It's a series of transformations from raw data to useful information.

Thinking in Transformations

Remember our coffee example? Let's take that transformation thinking a step further. When you make coffee, you're really doing a series of smaller transformations: beans to grounds, water to hot water, grounds and hot water to brewed coffee, brewed coffee to filtered coffee. Each step is its own clean, well-defined transformation.

This is exactly how functional programmers think about problems. Instead of diving straight into how to solve something, they first break it down into a series of transformations. Let's see this in action with a real-world example.

Imagine you're building a text analysis tool for a writing app. The app needs to take a document and generate a summary of its reading statistics: word count, average word length, most common words, etc. Here's how a functional thinker would approach this:

```
analyzeText :: Text -> TextStats
analyzeText =
    splitIntoWords
    >>> removeStopWords
    >>> analyze
    where
        analyze = parallel [countWords,
            calculateAverageLength, findMostCommon 10]
```

See what we did there? Instead of thinking about loops and counters, we thought about how our data transforms from one shape to another. The document is just text that flows through a series of transformations, each one creating a new form of that data.

For comparison, here's how many developers might approach this procedurally:

```python
def analyze_text(text):
    stats = {}
    words = text.split()
    filtered_words = []
    # Remove stop words
    for word in words:
        if word.lower() not in stop_words:
            filtered_words.append(word)
    # Count words
    stats['word_count'] = len(filtered_words)
    # Calculate average length
    total_length = 0
    for word in filtered_words:
        total_length += len(word)
    stats['avg_length'] = total_length / len(
        filtered_words)
    # Find common words
    word_freq = {}
    for word in filtered_words:
        word_freq[word] = word_freq.get(word, 0) + 1
    # Sort and get top 10
    stats['common_words'] = sorted(word_freq.items(),
        key=lambda x: x[1], reverse=True)[:10]
    return stats
```

The procedural version isn't bad code, but notice how it mixes different concerns. Word counting, length calculation, and frequency analysis are all interleaved. The functional version, on the other hand, separates these transformations cleanly.

This transformation thinking gives us some powerful advantages:

1. **Composability:** Each transformation is a building block that we can rearrange or reuse. Want to analyze without removing stop words? Just remove that transformation. Need to add sentence complexity analysis? Add another transformation to the pipeline.

2. **Parallelization:** Notice that parallel in our code? When transformations are pure (they only depend on their inputs), we can run them in parallel without any extra work. The procedural version would need significant restructuring to achieve this.

3. **Testability:** Each transformation can be tested in isolation. We can verify that splitIntoWords correctly handles all edge cases without worrying about the rest of the pipeline.

4. **Readability:** The code tells us what it's doing, not how it's doing it. A new developer can understand the high-level flow without getting lost in implementation details.

Think about how you'd add new features to each version. Want to add readability scoring? In the functional version, it's just another transformation to compose. In the procedural version, you'd need to carefully insert new logic into the existing loop structure.

```
analyzeText :: Text -> TextStats
analyzeText =
    splitIntoWords
    >>> removeStopWords
    >>> analyze
    >>> addReadabilityScore
  where
      analyze = parallel [countWords,
          calculateAverageLength, findMostCommon 10]
```

This is the power of thinking in transformations. Your code becomes a series of clear, composable steps that transform data from one shape to another. Each transformation is simple and focused, but together they can solve complex problems elegantly.

The Beauty of Immutability

Imagine you're at a restaurant with friends, sharing a pizza. Someone reaches over and takes a slice – that pizza has now changed state. If another friend arrives late and asks "How many slices were there?" the current state of the pizza doesn't tell the whole story. This is the world of mutable state, where things change over time, and history gets lost.

Now imagine instead that every time someone wants a slice, the waiter brings a new pizza with one fewer slice. Silly in the real world? Absolutely. But in the world of functional programming, this "create new instead of modifying" approach unlocks a world of clarity and reliability.

Let's see a concrete example. Here's a common task: updating a user's profile in a system:

```python
# The mutable approach
def update_user_profile(user, new_data):
    user.name = new_data.get('name', user.name)
    user.email = new_data.get('email', user.email)
    if 'address' in new_data:
        user.address.street =
            new_data['address'].get('street',
                                    user.address.street)
        user.address.city =
            new_data['address'].get('city',
                                    user.address.city)
    user.last_updated = datetime.now()
    db.save(user)
```

This code is modifying the user object in place. Seems straightforward, right? But what if another part of your system is trying to read this user's data at the same time? What if there's an error halfway through the update? What if you need to know what changed for audit purposes?

Here's the functional, immutable approach:

```
updateUserProfile :: User -> ProfileUpdate -> (User,
    AuditLog)
updateUserProfile user update =
    let newAddress =
            updateAddress (address user) (
                addressUpdate update)
        newUser = User {
            name = fromMaybe (name user) (updateName
                update)
            , email = fromMaybe (email user) (
                updateEmail update)
            , address = newAddress
            , lastUpdated = getCurrentTime
            }
        auditLog = createAuditLog user newUser
    in (newUser, auditLog)
```

Instead of modifying the existing user, we create a new user record with the updated values. The original user remains unchanged. This might seem wasteful – why create a new object when we could just update the old one? But this immutability gives us several superpowers:

- **Time Travel Debugging:** Because we never modify existing data, we can keep a history of all states. Debugging becomes easier because we can reconstruct exactly what happened and when.

```
type UserHistory = [User]

updateWithHistory :: UserHistory -> ProfileUpdate
    -> UserHistory
updateWithHistory history update =
    let (newUser, _) = updateUserProfile (head
        history) update
    in newUser : history
```

- **Concurrency Without Locks:** Multiple parts of your system can safely work with the same data because they can't interfere with each other's copies.

- **Easier Testing:** When functions don't modify their inputs, tests become more predictable. You can run them in any order without worrying about state pollution.

- **Automatic Audit Trails:** Since we're creating new versions instead of modifying existing ones, we naturally have before and after snapshots of every change.

But perhaps the biggest benefit is peace of mind. With immutable data, a whole class of bugs simply cannot exist. No more "who changed this value?" or "when did this get modified?" The data you have is the data you have, period.

Of course, at some point, data does need to change – users update their profiles, orders get processed, messages get sent. The trick is to push these changes to the edges of your system. Your core business logic operates on immutable data, and only at the boundaries (like database writes or API calls) do you deal with state changes.

Think of it like a photo editor. Instead of modifying the original photo, each edit creates a new version. You can always go back to previous versions, try different combinations of edits, or share the original while still working on changes. Your edits are transformations that create new photos rather than mutations that modify the original.

This mindset shift – from modifying things in place to creating new versions with changes – is another key aspect of the functional mind. Combined with our transformation thinking, it leads to code that's not just more reliable, but more understandable. Each transformation takes immutable data as input and produces new immutable data as output, creating a clear flow of data through your system.

A Quick Tour of Haskell

Before diving into real-world examples, let's take a moment to understand the basic syntax and concepts of Haskell. Don't worry – you won't need to become an expert, but understanding a few key concepts will help you follow the examples.

Haskell is a purely functional programming language, which means it enforces functional principles strictly. This makes it an excellent language for learning functional thinking, as it prevents us from falling back into procedural habits.

Types and Functions

In Haskell, everything starts with types. They're like contracts that tell us what a function expects and what it returns:

```
-- This says: takeFirstName takes a Person and returns
   a String
takeFirstName :: Person -> String
takeFirstName person = firstName person

-- A function that takes two arguments
add :: Int -> Int -> Int
add x y = x + y

-- A function that might not return a value
findUser :: UserId -> Maybe User
findUser id =     -- returns Just user or Nothing
```

The :: symbol means "has type of". That arrow -> shows

what goes in and what comes out. It's like saying "this transforms into that".

In Haskell, functions are "curried" by default, meaning a function that takes multiple arguments is actually a sequence of functions that each take one argument

Therefore, in the second function shown above, the type signature add `::` `Int` `->` `Int` `->` Int can be read as: "add is a function that takes an integer and returns a function that takes another integer and returns an integer".

The **Maybe** type in Haskell is used for cases where a function might not find or return a valid result. It is a common pattern in Haskell for safe handling of operations that might fail, avoiding null references or exceptions.

Lists and Operations

Lists are everywhere in functional programming. Here's how we work with them:

```haskell
-- Creating lists
numbers = [1, 2, 3, 4, 5]

-- map applies a function to each element
doubled = map (*2) numbers   -- results in [2, 4, 6, 8,
    10]

-- filter keeps elements that satisfy a condition
evens = filter even numbers   -- results in [2, 4]

-- Common patterns you'll see
```

```
names = ["Alice", "Bob", "Charlie"]
upperNames = map toUpper names
longNames = filter (\name -> length name > 4) names
```

In the last line of above code, the filter uses a lambda function (anonymous function), which takes a parameter *name*, returns *True* if the length of *name* is greater than 4, returns *False* otherwise.

Pattern Matching

Pattern matching is a powerful way to handle different cases. It's like a super-powered switch statement:

```
data Shape =
    Circle Float          -- radius
    | Rectangle Float Float   -- width and height

area :: Shape -> Float
area shape = case shape of
    Circle r -> pi * r * r
    Rectangle w h -> w * h
```

The above *area* function uses pattern matching with *case* to return πr^2 for a Circle shape, or w*h for a Rectangle shape. This is similar to the concept of polymorphism in Object Oriented Programming.

Common Operators

You'll see these operators frequently in our examples:

```
-- >>> chains functions (like a pipeline)
processData = step1 >>> step2 >>> step3

-- >>= chains operations that might fail
validateUser = checkEmail >>= checkPassword >>=
    checkAge

-- <$> applies a function to a wrapped value
uppercase <$> getName   -- if getName returns Maybe
    String

-- where lets us define local functions
calculateStats data = result
    where
        step1 = -- some calculation
        step2 = -- another calculation
        result = step2 (step1 data)
```

These are common Haskell patterns for:

- Function composition (»>)

- Error handling (»=)

- Container manipulation (<$>)

- Local scoping (where)

Note that the <$> operation also called fmap, which can be thought as "if there's a value inside, apply this function to it, keeping the container intact."

Maybe and Either: Handling Optional Values and Errors

```haskell
-- Maybe: for optional values
data Maybe a = Just a | Nothing

findUser :: Id -> Maybe User
findUser id =
    if userExists id
        then Just (lookupUser id)
        else Nothing

-- Either: for error handling
data Either error value = Left error | Right value
-- Left and Right are constructors:
-- Left (error) holds an error value; Right (value)
--    holds a successful value

validateAge :: Int -> Either String Int
validateAge age =
    if age >= 0 && age < 150
        then Right age
        else Left "Age must be between 0 and 150"
```

Putting It All Together

Here's a simple but complete example bringing these concepts together:

```haskell
-- Define our types
data User = User { name :: String, age :: Int }
data UserError =
    InvalidAge
    | NameTooShort
    | EmptyUserList
    deriving Show

-- Transform functions
toUpperCase :: String -> String
toUpperCase = map toUpper

addTitle :: String -> String
addTitle name = "Mr./Ms. " ++ name

-- Validation functions returning Either
validateAge :: Int -> Either UserError Int
validateAge age
    | age < 0      = Left InvalidAge
    | age > 150    = Left InvalidAge
    | otherwise    = Right age

validateName :: String -> Either UserError String
validateName name
    | length name < 2 = Left NameTooShort
    | otherwise       = Right name

-- Safe constructor returning Either
makeUser :: String -> Int -> Either UserError User
makeUser name age = do
    validatedName <- validateName name
    validatedAge <- validateAge age
    Right $ User validatedName validatedAge
```

```haskell
-- Find user by name returning Maybe
findUser :: String -> [User] -> Maybe User
findUser searchName = find (\user -> name user ==
    searchName)


-- Process users with error handling
processUsers :: [User] -> Either UserError [String]
processUsers users = do
    -- Check for empty list
    if null users
        then Left EmptyUserList
        else Right users
    >>= \validUsers -> Right $ validUsers
        & filter isAdult
        & map getName
        & map (toUpperCase . addTitle)  -- Composed
                transformations

    where
        isAdult user = age user >= 18
        getName user = name user


-- Example usage function showing <$> operations
example :: IO ()
example = do
    -- Try to create some users
    let user1 = makeUser "Alice" 20
        user2 = makeUser "Bob" 16
        user3 = makeUser "Charlie" 25


    -- Using <$> with Maybe
    let foundUser = findUser "Alice" [User "Alice" 20,
        User "Bob" 16]
```

```haskell
putStrLn "Maybe examples:"
print $ toUpperCase <$> (name <$> foundUser)     --
    Just "ALICE"
print $ addTitle <$> (name <$> foundUser)        --
    Just "Mr./Ms. Alice"

-- Using <$> with Either
putStrLn "\nEither examples:"
print $ toUpperCase <$> validateName "Alice"     --
    Right "ALICE"
print $ addTitle <$> validateName "Bob"          --
    Right "Mr./Ms. Bob"

-- Combining transformations with <$>
putStrLn "\nCombined transformations:"
print $ (addTitle . toUpperCase) <$> (name <$>
    foundUser)   -- Just "Mr./Ms. ALICE"

-- Process valid users
case sequence [user1, user3] of
    Left err -> putStrLn $ "Error: " ++ show err
    Right validUsers -> do
        let result = processUsers validUsers
        case result of
            Left err -> putStrLn $ "Error: " ++
                show err
            Right names -> do
                putStrLn "\nProcessed names:"
                mapM_ putStrLn names

                -- Transform Maybe User with <$>
                let maybeUser = findUser "Alice"
                    validUsers
```

```
putStrLn "\nTransformed user name;"
print $ toUpperCase <$> (name <$>
    maybeUser)
```

Don't worry if you don't grasp all the details – the key is understanding that functional programming is about:

- Defining clear types for your data

- Writing functions that transform data from one type to another

- Composing these functions into pipelines

- Using patterns like Maybe and Either to handle edge cases

With this foundation, you'll be better equipped to understand the real-world examples in the next section, where we'll see these concepts applied to solving practical problems.

Real-world Examples in Haskell

Let's move beyond toy examples and see how functional thinking solves real-world problems. We'll look at three scenarios
that many developers face regularly, and see how functional programming transforms these challenges into elegant solutions.

Case 1: Real-time Data Processing Pipeline

Imagine you're building a system that processes streaming financial market data. You need to ingest trades, convert currencies,
detect patterns, and generate alerts – all in real-time. Here's how
it might look:

```haskell
type Trade = (Symbol, Price, Volume, Currency)
type Alert = (Symbol, AlertType, String)

processMarketData :: Stream Trade -> Stream Alert
processMarketData =
    normalize                 -- Normalize all trades to
        USD
    >>> windowTrades 5        -- Group trades in 5-minute
        windows
    >>> detectPatterns        -- Look for specific
        patterns
    >>> generateAlerts        -- Convert patterns to
        alerts
    where
        normalize = mapStream convertToUSD
        windowTrades minutes = chunksOf (minutes * 60)
```

```
detectPatterns = mapStream
    findSuspiciousActivity
```

The beauty here isn't just in the concise code – it's in how naturally it models the problem. Each step is a transformation of the data stream, and the whole pipeline reads like a description of what we want, not how to do it.

Case 2: Complex Form Validation

Web developers often struggle with form validation logic becoming a tangled mess. Here's how functional programming can make it clear and maintainable:

```
data FormData = FormData {
    email :: Text,
    password :: Text,
    age :: Int
}

validate :: FormData -> Either [Error] ValidatedForm
validate form =
    validateAll [
        validateEmail (email form),
        validatePassword (password form),
        validateAge (age form)
    ]

-- Each validation returns Either Error a
validateEmail :: Text -> Either Error Email
validateEmail =
    checkNotEmpty
```

```
>=> checkValidFormat        -- >=> is function
    composition with Either
>=> checkDomainExists

validatePassword :: Text -> Either Error Password
validatePassword =
    checkNotEmpty
    >=> checkLength 8
    >=> checkComplexity
```

Notice how each validation is independent and composable. We can easily add new validations or change the order without affecting the others. The Either type elegantly handles success and failure cases.

Case 3: Event-Driven Architecture

Many modern applications use event-driven architectures. Functional programming excels at processing streams of events:

```
data Event =
    UserRegistered User
    | OrderPlaced Order
    | PaymentReceived Payment

processEvents :: Stream Event -> Stream Action
processEvents =
    classify              -- Group related events
    >>> correlate         -- Find relationships between
        events
    >>> decide            -- Determine required actions
    where
```

```
classify = groupBy eventType
correlate = mapStream findRelatedEvents
decide events = case events of
    [UserRegistered user, OrderPlaced order]
        ->
        SendWelcomeEmail user
    [OrderPlaced order, PaymentReceived
        payment] ->
        ProcessOrder order
    _ -> NoAction
```

This code clearly shows how events flow through the system and how different combinations of events trigger different actions. The pattern matching in the decide function makes it easy to add new event combinations.

These examples demonstrate how functional programming scales to real-world complexity:

- **Data Pipelines:** Transformation-based thinking naturally models data flow, making it perfect for processing streams of data in real-time.

- **Validation Logic:** By composing small, pure functions, we can build complex validation rules that are easy to understand and modify.

- **Event Processing:** Pattern matching and immutable data make it natural to handle complex event scenarios, while keeping the code readable and maintainable.

What makes these solutions particularly powerful is how they maintain clarity even as requirements grow. Each piece is isolated and composable, allowing us to build complex systems from simple, understandable parts.

Stories of Functional Solutions in Industry

Let's explore some real success stories where functional programming solved critical business problems. These examples demonstrate how functional thinking scales to enterprise challenges, though I should mention that the code we'll look at is based on my approximation and simplified for clarity. Think of these examples as sketches that capture the essence of the solutions – the actual production systems are naturally more complex, with additional layers handling everything from monitoring to integration. But the core ideas and patterns we'll discuss are very much real and battle-tested. They've helped teams at major companies tackle thorny problems in elegant ways. So while we won't be looking at exact production code, we'll see authentic approaches that you could adapt for your own challenges.

Facebook's Spam Fighting System

Facebook developed a spam detection system using Haskell. The key challenge was processing millions of posts in real-time while maintaining system reliability. Here's a simplified version of how such a system might work:

```
data Content = Post Text | Comment Text | Message Text
data SpamVerdict = Safe | Suspicious | Spam

detectSpam :: Stream Content -> Stream (Content,
    SpamVerdict)
detectSpam =
```

```
classify                 -- Initial
  classification
>>> enrichWithMetadata    -- Add user history, IP
  info, etc.
>>> applyMLModel          -- Run through ML model
>>> determineVerdict      -- Make final decision
where
    classify = mapStream initialClassification
    enrichWithMetadata = mapStreamAsync
        fetchMetadata
    determineVerdict = mapStream makeDecision
```

The functional approach made it easier to:

- Process content in parallel

- Handle failures gracefully

- Update rules without system restarts

- Maintain audit trails of decisions

Jane Street's Trading Systems

While we can't show their actual code, we can illustrate how functional programming helps manage complex trading logic:

```
data Order = Order {
    symbol :: Symbol,
    price :: Price,
    quantity :: Quantity,
    constraints :: [TradeConstraint]
}
```

```
validateAndExecute :: Order -> Market -> Either Error
    Transaction
validateAndExecute order market = do
    -- Chain of validations and transformations
    validOrder <- validateOrder order
    price <- determinePrice validOrder market
    risk <- calculateRisk price market
    if acceptableRisk risk
        then executeOrder validOrder price
        else Left RiskTooHigh
```

This approach helps traders:

- Catch errors before they become costly mistakes

- Audit every step of the trading process

- Quickly adapt to market conditions

- Test strategies without risking real money

WhatsApp's Message Processing

WhatsApp handles billions of messages daily. Here's how a functional approach might handle message processing:

```
data Message = Message {
    content :: Content,
    metadata :: Metadata,
    routing :: RoutingInfo
}
```

```
processMessage :: Message -> IO [Action]
processMessage msg = do
    let actions = concat [
            validateMessage msg,
            determineRecipients msg,
            applyPrivacyRules msg,
            generateNotifications msg
        ]
    sequence $ filter isUrgent actions
```

Key benefits include:

* Predictable message handling

* Easy to add new features

* Reliable delivery guarantees

* Clear audit trails

Common Patterns of Success

These stories share several themes:

* Scalability Through Immutability

```
-- Each transformation creates new data instead
   of modifying
type Pipeline a b = Stream a -> Stream b

process :: Pipeline InputData OutputData
process = transform1 >>> transform2 >>>
    transform3
```

- Reliable Error Handling

```
data Result a =
    Success a
    | Retry Int a       -- Retry count and data
    | Failure Error

handleRequest :: Request -> Result Response
handleRequest req =
    case validateRequest req of
        Left err -> Failure err
        Right valid -> processValidRequest valid
```

- Easy Testing and Verification

```
-- Pure functions are easy to test
prop_alwaysValid :: Order -> Bool
prop_alwaysValid order =
    case validateOrder order of
        Left _ -> True          -- Invalid orders
                                    caught
        Right valid -> checkInvariants valid
```

These success stories demonstrate that functional programming isn't just an academic exercise – it's a powerful tool for building robust, maintainable systems at scale. The initial investment in learning functional thinking pays off in:

- Fewer production bugs

- Easier maintenance

- Better testing

- More confident deployments

- Clearer code documentation

Most importantly, these stories show that functional programming can handle the messiness of real-world requirements while maintaining code clarity and reliability.

Here's a more conversational rewrite:

Conclusion: The Functional Power

Let's take a moment to reflect on our journey through functional programming. From our first steps with Haskell to exploring real-world applications, we've seen how this paradigm isn't just an academic curiosity – it's a powerful tool that's reshaping how we build software.

Why Functional Programming Matters Now

You might be wondering, "Why should I care about functional programming today?" Well, look at the challenges we're facing in modern software development. We're building systems that need to handle massive amounts of data, run operations in parallel, and maintain reliability at scale. Sound familiar? These are exactly the kinds of problems where functional programming shines.

Think about the current trends in our industry. We're all talking about immutable infrastructure, stateless microservices, and event-driven architectures. Notice something? These concepts align beautifully with functional principles. It's as if the industry has been gradually discovering what functional programmers have known all along!

Making the Transition

Now, I know what you're thinking: "This all sounds great, but how do I actually start?" Don't worry – you don't need to rewrite your entire codebase in Haskell overnight. Start small. Look at this simple example:

```
-- Begin with simple transformations
processUsers =
    filter isActive
    >>> map normalize
    >>> sort
```

See how readable that is? It's almost like reading English: filter the active users, normalize them, and sort them. This is the beauty of functional thinking–it lets us express our intentions clearly.

Focus on understanding the core concepts first. Immutability, pure functions, composition, and type safety might seem like abstract terms, but they're your friends in building reliable software. Think of them as guardrails that keep you on the right path.

And here's a secret: you can start applying these ideas in whatever language you're using right now. Pick a small piece of your code, maybe some data processing logic, and try rewriting it with functional principles. Small wins build confidence.

The Future is Functional

Let me be clear – I'm not saying every project needs to be written in Haskell. That's not the point. What I am saying is that functional thinking is becoming an essential skill for every developer.

Think about it: when was the last time you had to break down a complex problem into smaller pieces? Or handle errors in a clean way? Or build a system that needs to handle multiple operations simultaneously? These are all scenarios where functional thinking gives you powerful tools.

Remember how we started this book talking about declaring what we want rather than how to do it? Functional programming lets us do exactly that. It's not just about writing code differently – it's about thinking differently. And in today's world of increasing complexity, this different way of thinking isn't just useful – it's essential.

The functional approach gives us code that's easier to understand, test, and maintain. It helps us handle complexity with grace. And most importantly, it brings us closer to expressing our intentions directly to the computer, bridging the gap between what we want and how we tell the computer to do it.

Functional programming is not just another programming paradigm – it's a powerful way of thinking about software development that addresses many of the challenges we face in building modern systems. Whether you're processing financial transactions, fighting spam, or building the next big messaging platform, functional thinking can help you build better, more reliable software.

The journey from understanding map and filter to building robust, scalable systems might seem long, but each step builds naturally on the last. The investment in learning functional programming pays dividends in code quality, maintainability, and developer confidence.

Remember: The goal isn't to rewrite everything in Haskell, but to enhance your problem-solving toolkit with functional thinking. Start small, think in transformations, and let the elegance of functional programming guide you to better solutions.

Looking Ahead: The Logical Mind

As we conclude our exploration of functional programming, we're naturally led to an even deeper aspect of computer science: logic and reasoning. While functional programming teaches us to think in terms of transformations and pure functions, logical programming takes us further into the realm of mathematical reasoning and formal proof.

In the next chapter, "The Logical Mind," we'll discover how programming languages like Prolog and tools like theorem provers allow us to express problems in terms of logical relationships and let the computer deduce solutions. We'll see how this paradigm, though different from functional programming, shares its roots in mathematical rigor and clear thinking.

If functional programming shows us how to compose simple functions to solve complex problems, logical programming will show us how to state what we want and let the computer figure out how to achieve it. Let's begin this fascinating journey into the world of logical reasoning.

The Logical Mind

Have you ever watched Sherlock Holmes solve a case? He doesn't just randomly try different solutions. Instead, he gathers facts, establishes relationships between them, and uses logical deduction to reach conclusions. "When you have eliminated the impossible," he famously says, "whatever remains, however improbable, must be the truth."

This is exactly how logic programming works. It's a way of telling computers to think like a detective – not by trying random solutions or following step-by-step instructions, but by reasoning about facts and relationships to deduce answers.

Thinking in Relations and Rules

Let's start with a mental shift. Instead of thinking about how to compute something, think about what is true about your problem. Imagine you're organizing a dinner party. You know that:

- John is allergic to seafood

- Mary is vegetarian

- Tom will eat anything

- Pizza contains cheese

- Sushi contains seafood

Now, instead of writing a program to match people with foods, you can simply state these facts and ask questions like "What can John eat?" A logic program will figure out the answer by reasoning about the relationships between people and foods.

This is fundamentally different from how most of us are used to programming. We're not writing instructions like "check each food, if it contains seafood then remove it from John's options." Instead, we're stating facts about the world and letting the computer reason about them.

Think about how you'd solve a murder mystery. You don't start with a procedure; you start with facts:

- The crime happened at 9 PM

- The butler was in the garden

- The cook was in the kitchen

- Only someone with a key could enter the study

- Only the butler and cook had keys

Now, instead of writing a program to match people with foods, you can simply state these facts and ask questions like "What can John eat?" A logic program will figure out the answer by reasoning about the relationships between people and foods.

This is fundamentally different from how most of us are used to programming. We're not writing instructions like "check each food, if it contains seafood then remove it from John's options." Instead, we're stating facts about the world and letting the computer reason about them.

Think about how you'd solve a murder mystery. You don't start with a procedure; you start with facts:

- The crime happened at 9 PM

- The butler was in the garden

- The cook was in the kitchen

- Only someone with a key could enter the study

- Only the butler and cook had keys

From these facts, a logic program can deduce possible suspects, just like a detective would. This is the essence of logic programming – stating what we know and letting the computer draw conclusions.

The beauty of this approach is that it mirrors how we naturally think about many problems. When you're figuring out your schedule, you don't run through a series of steps – you think about constraints and relationships:

- Meetings must be during work hours

- Can't have two meetings at the same time

- Team members must be available

- Some meetings require specific rooms

Logic programming lets us express these natural constraints directly, without having to figure out how to schedule everything. We just state what must be true, and the computer figures out a solution that satisfies all our requirements.

This way of thinking – in terms of relationships and rules rather than steps and procedures – opens up new possibilities for solving problems. It's particularly powerful for problems that involve complex relationships, constraints, or deductive reasoning.

How Prolog Thinks Like a Detective

Picture our favorite detective again. When Sherlock Holmes investigates a case, he doesn't follow a predetermined set of steps. Instead, he:

1. Collects facts from witnesses and evidence

2. Makes connections between these facts

3. Follows leads, backtracking when a line of inquiry proves fruitless

4. Keeps trying different theories until finding one that explains all the evidence

This is exactly how **Prolog**, our logic programming language, approaches problems. Let me show you a simple mystery to illustrate this:

Imagine we're investigating who ate the cookies from the cookie jar. We know:

- The cookie thief had chocolate on their fingers

- Only someone who was in the kitchen could have reached the cookie jar

- Alice had chocolate on her fingers and was seen in the garden

- Bob had chocolate on his fingers and was seen in the kitchen

- Charlie had clean hands and was in the kitchen

A traditional program would need specific instructions about how to find the culprit. But with logic programming, we just state these facts and ask "Who took the cookies?" Prolog thinks like this:

"Let's see... who could have done it? I need someone who:

1. Had chocolate on their fingers (that's Alice and Bob)

2. Was in the kitchen (that's Bob and Charlie)

3. Satisfies BOTH conditions... Aha! Only Bob meets all the criteria!"

What's fascinating is that if we discover new information – say, a secret passage from the garden to the kitchen – Prolog automatically adjusts its reasoning without us having to change any procedures. The detective (Prolog) simply incorporates the new fact into its reasoning.

This detective-like thinking is particularly powerful when the solution isn't straightforward. Suppose we're solving a more complex mystery:

- Someone broke into the safe

- The safe could only be opened with a key or by knowing the combination

- Only senior staff knew the combination

- Only security had keys

- The break-in happened during night shift

- During night shift, only junior staff and security were present

Prolog approaches this like a real detective, systematically exploring possibilities and eliminating contradictions. It might first try assuming a junior staff member did it, realize they couldn't have known the combination, backtrack, and then consider security personnel who had keys.

This ability to backtrack – to say "this line of reasoning didn't work, let me try another approach" – is one of the most powerful features of logic programming. It's like Sherlock Holmes following a lead, realizing it doesn't fit all the evidence, and then exploring a different theory.

Most importantly, we never had to tell Prolog "how" to solve these mysteries. We just described "what" we know, and it figured out the solution through logical deduction – just like a good detective would.

Knowledge Representation Logically

Think about how you store knowledge in your mind. When I ask you "What's a bird?" you don't run through a program – instead, you access a web of interconnected facts: birds have feathers, most birds can fly, birds lay eggs, some birds are pets, penguins are birds but can't fly... It's all about relationships and exceptions, not procedures and steps.

This is exactly how we represent knowledge in logic programming. Instead of writing instructions about how to process information, we create a network of facts and relationships that mirror how we naturally think about things.

Let's take a simple example from a family tree:

```
parent(anna, bob).      % Anna is Bob's parent
parent(bob, carol).     % Bob is Carol's parent
female(anna).           % Anna is female
female(carol).          % Carol is female
male(bob).              % Bob is male
```

Notice how natural this feels – we're just stating things we know to be true. We can then add rules that capture more complex relationships:

```
grandmother(X, Z) :- parent(X, Y), parent(Y, Z),
    female(X).
```

This reads almost like English: "X is the grandmother of Z if X is a parent of Y, Y is a parent of Z, and X is female." We're not telling the computer "how" to find grandmothers – we're just describing "what" a grandmother is.

Real-world knowledge is often much messier, full of exceptions and special cases. Consider representing knowledge about vehicles:

- Cars are vehicles

- Cars usually have four wheels

- But some specialized cars have three wheels

- Vehicles need fuel to run

- But electric vehicles use electricity, not gasoline

- A vehicle can't be in two places at once

- Unless it's a quantum particle (but that's another story!)

Logic programming handles these complexities naturally. We can express both general rules and exceptions without getting tangled in procedural code. It's like building a model of how things work in the real world, rather than writing instructions for handling every possible case.

This approach becomes powerful when dealing with real-world knowledge bases. Imagine a medical diagnosis system:

- Symptoms suggest possible conditions

- Conditions have risk factors

- Medications have contraindications

- Treatments have prerequisites

- Some combinations of medications are dangerous

By representing this knowledge as logical relationships rather than procedural code, we can:

- Add new medical knowledge without rewriting existing code

- Let the system reason about complex combinations of symptoms

- Automatically detect potentially dangerous drug interactions

- Explain its reasoning by showing the chain of logical deductions

The beauty of this approach is that it separates "what" we know from "how" we use that knowledge. Just like a human expert, the system can apply its knowledge to new situations without needing new instructions.

Understanding Prolog: A Brief Tour

Before we dive deeper into solving puzzles and business problems, let's take a quick tour of Prolog, the most popular logic programming language. Don't worry – this won't be a dry technical manual. Think of Prolog as a new language that expresses relationships and rules in a way that's closer to how we naturally think.

Facts: Stating What We Know

Let's start with the foundation of Prolog programming: facts. Facts are the building blocks of our program's knowledge – simple, direct statements about what's true in our world. Think of it as creating a tiny universe of information:

```prolog
% Simple facts about people and their preferences
likes(john, pizza).        % John likes pizza
likes(mary, sushi).        % Mary likes sushi
likes(john, ice_cream).    % John also likes ice cream
friend(john, mary).        % John and Mary are friends
friend(mary, alice).       % Mary and Alice are friends
student(john).             % John is a student
teacher(alice).            % Alice is a teacher
teaches(alice, math).      % Alice teaches math
enrolled(john, math).      % John is enrolled in math
```

Each fact is like a simple declaration about our world. Notice the elegant simplicity – there's no complex syntax, just straightforward statements that read almost like English. The period at the end of each line is like saying "this is definitely true, full stop!"

Facts can represent any kind of information: relationships between people, properties of objects, or any concrete piece of knowledge. They're our program's axioms – the basic truths from which everything else will follow.

Rules: Expressing Relationships

Now comes the truly powerful part: rules. While facts tell us what is true, rules tell us how to discover new truths from what we already know. They're like logical recipes that combine facts to create new insights:

```
% If X likes Y and Y likes X, they're mutual fans
mutual_fans(X, Y) :-
    likes(X, Y),
    likes(Y, X).

% Someone is happy if they're eating something they
    like
happy(Person) :-
    eating(Person, Food),
    likes(Person, Food).

% You can recommend food to someone if their friend
    likes it
recommend(Person, Food) :-
    friend(Person, Friend),
    likes(Friend, Food),
    \+ likes(Person, Food).  % Only recommend if they
```

```
         don't already like it

% Someone can help with homework if they're a teacher
   of the subject
can_help_with(Helper, Student, Subject) :-
    teacher(Helper),
    teaches(Helper, Subject),
    enrolled(Student, Subject).
```

See that :- symbol? It's like saying "is true if..." or "follows from..." The rules read almost like logical sentences:

- X and Y are mutual fans if X likes Y and Y likes X

- A person is happy if they're eating some food and they like that food

- You can recommend food to someone if their friend likes it and they don't already like it

- Someone can help with homework if they're a teacher of the subject and the student is enrolled in it

Each rule combines simpler facts or other rules to express more complex relationships. It's like building with logical LEGO blocks!

Queries: Asking Questions

This is where Prolog truly shines. Once we've built our world of facts and rules, we can ask questions about it. Queries are how we explore and discover what's true in our logical universe:

```
?- likes(john, pizza). % Is it true that John likes
    pizza?
true.

?- likes(X, sushi). % Who likes sushi?
X = mary.

?- happy(john). % Is John happy?
true. % (If we had a fact: eating(john, pizza))

?- recommend(john, Food). % What food might John like?
Food = sushi ; % Because Mary (his friend) likes sushi

?- can_help_with(Helper, john, math). % Who can help
    John with math?
Helper = alice. % Because Alice teaches math and John
    is enrolled
```

Each query (marked with ?-) is like asking Prolog to solve a puzzle using our facts and rules. The beauty is that we can ask very specific questions ("Does John like pizza?") or very open-ended ones ("Who likes what?"). Prolog will diligently search through all possible combinations of facts and rules to find answers.

We can even ask questions with multiple variables, and Prolog will find all possible combinations that make our query true. It's like having a tireless detective who can explore every possible logical connection in our knowledge base!

Variables and Pattern Matching

Let's talk about one of the most fascinating aspects of Prolog: how it handles variables and pattern matching. Unlike other programming languages where variables are just containers for values, Prolog variables are more like placeholders in a logical puzzle.

Here's something that might surprise you: in Prolog, any word that starts with a capital letter is a variable. It's like having a wildcard that can match anything. Think of it as leaving blanks in a sentence that can be filled in different ways.

Let's look at a practical example:

```
% Anyone who teaches is busy
busy(Person) :- teacher(Person).

% Anyone who has homework is busy
busy(Person) :- student(Person), has_homework(Person).

% Find all busy people
?- busy(Who).
Who = alice ;  % Because alice is a teacher
Who = john.    % If john has homework (since he's a
    student)
```

Look at how natural this reads! We're saying "a Person is busy if they're a teacher" and "a Person is busy if they're a student and they have homework." The variable Person acts like a fill-in-the-blank that Prolog will try to match with actual people.

Let's expand this example to see more of pattern matching in action:

```
teacher(alice).
student(john).
student(mary).
has_homework(john).
has_class_today(alice, math).
has_class_today(john, math).

% Find who's in the math class
?- has_class_today(Person, math).
Person = alice ;
Person = john.

% We can use variables in multiple places
same_class(Person1, Person2) :-
has_class_today(Person1, Class),
has_class_today(Person2, Class),
Person1 = Person2.
```

See how powerful this becomes?

When we write `has_class_today(Person, math)`, Person is like a blank space that Prolog will fill in with anyone who has a math class. We can use variables anywhere we want to say "I don't care what this is specifically, but it needs to match something."

This pattern matching is at the heart of how Prolog thinks. When you ask Prolog a question with variables, it tries to find all the ways those variables could be filled in to make your statement true. It's like having a detective who's really good at filling in the blanks!

Here's another cool thing: variables remember what they match within a single rule. So if you use the same variable name multiple times, it has to match the same thing each time. This is incredibly useful for finding connections:

```
% Finding people who share any class
classmate(StudentA, StudentB) :-
has_class_today(StudentA, SharedClass),  % Find a class
    for StudentA
has_class_today(StudentB, SharedClass),  % StudentB
    must have the SAME class
StudentA = StudentB.  % They can't be the same person
```

In this last example, SharedClass must be the same value in both places it appears. This is how we can find people who share classes – the variable acts like a bridge connecting the two conditions.

Think of Prolog variables as logical placeholders that help us express patterns and relationships. They're not just storage spaces for data – they're tools for describing what we're looking for. This is a key part of declarative programming: instead of telling the computer how to find something, we describe the pattern of what we want to find, using variables as our wildcards.

Lists: Handling Collections

Let's talk about lists in Prolog, which have a fascinating way of thinking about collections. In Prolog, we can write lists using square brackets, like this:

```
% Lists are written in square brackets
```

```
likes(john, [pizza, pasta, salad]).
```

Now, here's where it gets interesting. Prolog has a beautiful way of thinking about lists: every list is seen as having two parts – a head and a tail. The head is the first element, and the tail is... well, everything else! It's like thinking of a train: the engine is the head, and all the other cars make up the tail.

We can use this head-tail concept directly in our code:

```
% We can match parts of lists using the | operator
[Head|Tail] = [1, 2, 3, 4].
% Head = 1
% Tail = [2, 3, 4]
```

See that vertical bar | in [Head|Tail]? It's like telling Prolog, "Split this list into its first element and everything else." This isn't just a cute trick – it's a powerful way to process lists recursively. Think about it: every list is either empty or has a head and a tail. This simple observation leads to elegant solutions for many problems.

Here's a classic example that shows this concept in action:

```
% A simple rule to check if something is in a list
member(X, [X|]). % If X is the head, we found it!
member(X, [|Tail]) :- member(X, Tail). % If not, look
    in the tail
```

This member predicate is saying: "Either X is the head of the list (first rule), or it's a member of the tail (second rule)." Notice how naturally the head-tail structure leads to recursive solutions? This is declarative thinking at its finest–we're describing what it means to be a member of a list, not how to search through one.

The Power of Backtracking

Now, let me share with you one of my favorite features of Prolog–something that makes it feel almost magical. It's called backtracking, and it's Prolog's superpower for finding multiple solutions to a problem.

Think about how we usually write programs. In most languages, when we ask for an answer, we get one answer and that's it. But real-world problems often have multiple valid solutions. This is where Prolog shines. Let's look at a simple example:

```
teaches(alice, math).
teaches(bob, history).
teaches(alice, physics).

?- teaches(Teacher, Subject).
```

When you run this query, something fascinating happens. Prolog doesn't just give you one answer and stop–it remembers all the possible paths it could take. Press semicolon (;), and it'll cheerfully offer another solution. Press period (.), and it'll stop. It's like having a conversation with your database!

```
Teacher = alice, Subject = math ;
Teacher = bob, Subject = history ;
Teacher = alice, Subject = physics.
```

But this isn't just a neat party trick. Think about real-world problems: finding all possible routes between cities, discovering all valid solutions to a puzzle, or identifying all students who meet certain criteria. Prolog's backtracking makes these problems surprisingly straightforward to solve.

Here's another example to drive this home:

```
likes(john, pizza).
likes(john, sushi).
likes(mary, sushi).
likes(mary, salad).

friends(X, Y) :- likes(X, Food), likes(Y, Food), X = Y
    .

?- friends(Who, WithWhom).
Who = john, WithWhom = mary ;
Who = mary, WithWhom = john.
```

In this case, we're finding pairs of friends who share food preferences. Prolog automatically backtracks through all possibilities, finding every pair of people who like the same food. Notice how we didn't need to write any loops or complex control structures? We just declared what it means to be friends (sharing a food preference), and Prolog figures out all the valid combinations.

This is where declarative programming really shows its strength. Instead of telling the computer how to search through combinations, we simply describe what we're looking for. The backtracking mechanism handles all the complexity of finding multiple solutions for us. It's like having a tireless assistant who's willing to explore every possibility until they've found all valid answers.

Remember: when you're using Prolog, you're not just getting one answer–you're getting all possible answers. This changes how you think about problem-solving. Instead of worrying about how to find solutions, you can focus on describing what makes a valid solution. Prolog's backtracking will do the heavy lifting for you.

A Simple Example Putting It All Together

Let's bring everything we've learned together with a practical example. Imagine you're helping a university organize study groups. Instead of manually matching students, why not let Prolog do the work? Here's how we might approach this:

```
% First, let's state some facts about who studies what
studies(john, math).
studies(mary, math).
studies(peter, physics).
studies(susan, math).
studies(susan, physics).
```

These are our basic facts–simple statements about which student studies which subject. Notice how natural this feels? We're just telling Prolog "John studies math" in a way that's almost like English.

Now, let's think about what makes two students potential study buddies:

```
% Define when two students can study together
can_study_together(Student1, Student2) :-
    studies(Student1, Subject),
```

```
    studies(Student2, Subject),
    Student1 \= Student2.  % They can't be the same
        person!
```

This rule is beautiful in its simplicity. We're saying two students can study together if they study the same subject and aren't the same person. We didn't specify "how" to find these pairs – we just declared "what" makes two students compatible study partners.

But why stop at pairs? Let's find groups of three:

```
% Find groups of three students
study_group(S1, S2, S3) :-
    can_study_together(S1, S2),
    can_study_together(S2, S3),
    can_study_together(S1, S3),
    S1 @< S2, S2 @< S3.  % This clever bit prevents
        duplicate groups
```

This last part is where the magic happens. We're defining what makes a valid study group of three: everyone needs to be able to study together, and that mysterious-looking @< ensures we don't get the same group listed in different orders (like "john, mary, susan" and "susan, john, mary").

Try running a query:

```
?- study_group(Who, WithWhom1, WithWhom2).
```

Prolog will happily find all possible study groups that satisfy our conditions. No loops, no complex algorithms–just a clear description of what we want.

This example showcases the essence of declarative programming in Prolog. Look at how we built it up:

Simple facts about who studies what

* A rule defining compatible study partners

* A rule combining these to find study groups

It's like building with LEGO blocks – each piece is simple and understandable on its own, but together they create something powerful. We never had to tell Prolog "how" to search for these groups or "how" to match students. We just described "what" we were looking for, and Prolog figured out the rest.

This is the beauty of declarative programming: complex problems can often be solved by combining simple, clear descriptions of what we want. The computer handles all the detailed work of figuring out how to find the solutions. Isn't that a more natural way to think about problem-solving?

Solving Puzzles with Logical Thinking

Now that we understand Prolog's basics, let's see how it turns puzzle-solving into a fascinating exercise in logical thinking. We'll start with a simple mystery and gradually work our way up to more complex puzzles.

A Simple Mystery

Let's solve our cookie jar mystery from earlier, but this time with actual Prolog code:

```
% Facts about our mystery
location(alice, garden).
location(bob, kitchen).
location(charlie, kitchen).
has_chocolate_fingers(alice).
has_chocolate_fingers(bob).
clean_hands(charlie).

% Rules for solving the mystery
suspect(Person) :-
    has_chocolate_fingers(Person),      % Must have
        chocolate fingers
    location(Person, kitchen).          % Must have been
        in the kitchen

% Query: ?- suspect(Who).
% Result: Who = bob
```

See how naturally the logic flows? We're not telling Prolog

"how" to solve the mystery – we're just describing what makes someone a suspect.

The Einstein Puzzle (Simplified Version)

Remember those logic puzzles that start with clues like "The person who lives in the blue house is not the doctor" and "The gardener lives next to the teacher"? These puzzles can drive people crazy with their complexity, yet they perfectly demonstrate how logic programming shines. Instead of struggling with pen and paper, we can let logical reasoning do the heavy lifting.

Let's look at a simplified version of Einstein's famous puzzle:

- In a street with three houses

- A doctor, a teacher, and a gardener live there

- Each house is a different color: red, blue, and green

- The teacher lives in the blue house

- The gardener lives next to the doctor

- The doctor doesn't live in the red house

In Prolog, we could express this puzzle like this:

```
% Each position is 1, 2, or 3
position(1). position(2). position(3).

% Solution will be in the form: solution(DocPos,
    TeachPos, GardPos, RedPos, BluePos, GreenPos)
```

```
solve(Solution) :-
    Solution = solution(DocPos, TeachPos, GardPos,
        RedPos, BluePos, GreenPos),

    % Each person and color must be in a valid
    %    position
    position(DocPos), position(TeachPos), position(
        GardPos),
    position(RedPos), position(BluePos), position(
        GreenPos),

    % All positions must be different
    different([DocPos, TeachPos, GardPos]),
    different([RedPos, BluePos, GreenPos]),

    % Teacher lives in blue house
    TeachPos = BluePos,

    % Gardener lives next to doctor (difference of 1)
    abs(GardPos - DocPos) =:= 1,

    % Doctor doesn't live in red house
    DocPos \= RedPos.

% Helper predicate to ensure all elements in a list
%    are different
different([]).
different([H|T]) :-
    not(member(H, T)),
    different(T).

% Query: ?- solve(Solution).
% Result: Solution = solution(1,3,2,2,3,1)
```

When we run this, Prolog acts like a detective. It doesn't blindly try every possibility – it uses the constraints to narrow down the search. For instance, knowing the teacher is in the blue house immediately eliminates many possibilities.

Sudoku

Let's look at another classic puzzle: Sudoku. While a traditional program would need complex algorithms to solve Sudoku, in Prolog we can express it purely in terms of constraints:

```
:- use_module(library(clpfd)).  % For finite domain
    constraints

sudoku(Rows) :-
    length(Rows, 9),
    maplist(same_length(Rows), Rows),
    append(Rows, Vs), Vs ins 1..9,
    maplist(all_distinct, Rows),
    transpose(Rows, Columns),
    maplist(all_distinct, Columns),
    Rows = [A,B,C,D,E,F,G,H,I],
    blocks(A, B, C), blocks(D, E, F), blocks(G, H, I).

blocks([], [], []).
blocks([A,B,C|Bs1], [D,E,F|Bs2], [G,H,I|Bs3]) :-
    all_distinct([A,B,C,D,E,F,G,H,I]),
    blocks(Bs1, Bs2, Bs3).
```

The beauty here is that we're just stating the rules of Sudoku:

• Each cell contains a number from 1 to 9

- Each row must have distinct numbers

- Each column must have distinct numbers

- Each 3x3 block must have distinct numbers

For querying this program, you need to ask this way:

```
?- Rows = [[_,_,_,_,_,_,_,_,_],
           [_,_,_,_,_,_,_,_,_],
           [_,_,_,_,_,_,_,_,_],
           [_,_,_,_,_,_,_,_,_],
           [_,_,_,_,_,_,_,_,_],
           [_,_,_,_,_,_,_,_,_],
           [_,_,_,_,_,_,_,_,_],
           [_,_,_,_,_,_,_,_,_],
           [_,_,_,_,_,_,_,_,_]],
   sudoku(Rows),
   maplist(label, Rows).
```

The predicate `maplist(label, Rows)` is to force Prolog to find concrete values:

```
Rows = [[1, 2, 3, 4, 5, 6, 7, 8, 9],
        [4, 5, 6, 7, 8, 9, 1, 2, 3],
        [7, 8, 9, 1, 2, 3, 4, 5, 6],
        [2, 1, 4, 3, 6, 5, 8, 9, 7],
        [3, 6, 5, 8, 9, 7, 2, 1, 4],
        [8, 9, 7, 2, 1, 4, 3, 6, 5],
        [5, 3, 1, 6, 4, 2, 9, 7, 8],
        [6, 4, 2, 9, 7, 8, 5, 3, 1],
        [9, 7, 8, 5, 3, 1, 6, 4, 2]]
```

We don't tell Prolog "how" to solve it – we just describe

"what" makes a valid solution. This is the essence of declarative programming.

A More Complex Example: Schedule Planning

This approach becomes incredibly powerful for real-world scheduling problems. Consider a school class scheduling system:

```
% Facts about teachers and subjects
teaches(smith, math).
teaches(jones, physics).
teaches(brown, chemistry).

% Available time slots
time_slot(1, '9:00').
time_slot(2, '10:00').
time_slot(3, '11:00').

% Available rooms
room(lab1).
room(lab2).
room(classroom1).

% Some rooms are suitable for specific subjects
suitable_room(physics, lab1).
suitable_room(physics, lab2).
suitable_room(math, classroom1).
suitable_room(chemistry, lab1).
suitable_room(chemistry, lab2).

% Create a valid schedule
create_schedule(Schedule) :-
```

```
Schedule = [class(Subject1, Teacher1, Room1, Time1
    ),
            class(Subject2, Teacher2, Room2, Time2
                ),
            class(Subject3, Teacher3, Room3, Time3
                )],

% Assign teachers to subjects they can teach
teaches(Teacher1, Subject1),
teaches(Teacher2, Subject2),
teaches(Teacher3, Subject3),
all_different([Teacher1, Teacher2, Teacher3]),

% Assign time slots
time_slot(Time1, _),
time_slot(Time2, _),
time_slot(Time3, _),
all_different([Time1, Time2, Time3]),

% Assign suitable rooms
room(Room1), suitable_room(Subject1, Room1),
room(Room2), suitable_room(Subject2, Room2),
room(Room3), suitable_room(Subject3, Room3),

% No room can be used twice at the same time
\+ room_conflict(Schedule).

room_conflict([class(_, _, R, T)|Rest]) :-
    member(class(_, _, R, T), Rest).
room_conflict([_|Rest]) :-
    room_conflict(Rest).

% Query: ?- create_schedule(Schedule).
```

What's beautiful about this approach is how easily we can add new constraints. Need to ensure certain classes aren't back-to-back? Just add another rule. Want to make sure specific teachers have breaks between classes? Add another constraint.

The Power of Logical Thinking

After solving the cookie jar mystery, tackling Einstein's puzzle, cracking Sudoku, and handling class scheduling, you might wonder: "Beyond these examples, where else can this logical thinking approach take us?" This is where the real power of logic programming reveals itself.

The profound insight isn't just that we can solve puzzles with Prolog – it's recognizing that many real-world problems are essentially logical puzzles in disguise. Just as we deduced who took the cookie and figured out who owns which pet, we can apply the same thinking to pressing real-world challenges:

- Planning a wedding seating arrangement (think of it as a more complex version of our class scheduling problem, but with social dynamics as constraints)

- Creating a sports tournament schedule (structurally similar to our Sudoku puzzle, where each slot must satisfy multiple conditions)

- Organizing a conference program (like our class scheduling problem scaled up, with speakers instead of teachers)

- Allocating hospital resources (similar to Einstein's puzzle, but with doctors, nurses, and shifts as our variables)

The approach we've used throughout our examples applies beautifully to these real-world challenges:

1. Express what you know as facts (just like we stated who had access to the cookie jar)

2. Define the rules that must be satisfied (similar to our Sudoku rules about unique numbers)

3. Let Prolog's logical reasoning find valid solutions (the same power that helped us schedule classes)

This is why our journey through these puzzles has been more than just intellectual exercise – it's been preparation for tackling real-world problems. The logical thinking patterns we've practiced with cookie thieves and Einstein's riddles are the same ones that can help organize complex events, manage resources, and solve practical logistics challenges. The magic lies not in the puzzles themselves, but in recognizing that the world is full of problems waiting to be solved through logical reasoning.

Business Cases

Remember how we solved puzzles by stating facts and rules? Now let's step into the business world, where the stakes are higher and the puzzles are more complex – but surprisingly, the logical approach remains just as powerful. Let's explore how logic programming is quietly revolutionizing various aspects of business operations.

Supply Chain Optimization

Imagine you're managing a global supply chain with thousands of products moving between hundreds of locations. Sound complicated? Let's break it down like our earlier puzzles. Instead of "who owns which pet," we're asking "which products should go where, and when?"

Just as we defined rules for our Sudoku puzzle, we can express supply chain constraints:

- "Fresh products must reach stores within 48 hours"
- "Warehouse A can't handle more than 10,000 units"
- "Transport costs between cities follow these rules..."

The beauty is that Prolog can handle these complex relationships just like it handled our class scheduling problem – but now it's optimizing inventory levels, reducing transportation costs, and ensuring timely deliveries.

Consider this simplified supply chain scenario:

```prolog
% Facts: warehouses, stores, and distances
warehouse(chicago).
warehouse(atlanta).
store(detroit).
store(miami).
store(boston).

distance(chicago, detroit, 200).
distance(chicago, boston, 800).
distance(atlanta, miami, 300).
distance(atlanta, boston, 900).

capacity(chicago, 10000).
capacity(atlanta, 8000).

% Rules for optimal routing
valid_route(Warehouse, Store, Distance) :-
    warehouse(Warehouse),
    store(Store),
    distance(Warehouse, Store, Distance),
    Distance < 500.  % Maximum viable distance

% Finding all valid routes
find_routes(Routes) :-
    findall((W,S,D), valid_route(W,S,D), Routes).
```

Resource Allocation in Manufacturing

Remember our class scheduling challenge? Manufacturing resource allocation is similar, but instead of teachers and class-

rooms, we're dealing with machines, workers, and production lines. The constraints are more numerous:

- Machine capabilities and limitations

- Worker shifts and skills

- Production deadlines and priorities

- Maintenance schedules

Logic programming shines here because it can handle these interrelated constraints naturally, just as it handled the complex rules of Einstein's puzzle.

Here's a simple example of scheduling machine operations:

```
% Facts: machines and their capabilities
machine(press_1, stamping).
machine(mill_1, milling).
machine(drill_1, drilling).

% Job requirements and durations
job(part_a, [stamping, milling], 60).    % 60 minutes
job(part_b, [drilling, milling], 45).
job(part_c, [stamping, drilling], 30).

% Time slots (in minutes from start of day)
available_slot(0, 240).      % 4-hour morning slot
available_slot(240, 480).    % 4-hour afternoon slot

% Rules for valid scheduling
can_schedule(Job, Machine, StartTime, EndTime) :-
    job(Job, Requirements, Duration),
```

```
machine(Machine, Operation),
member(Operation, Requirements),
available_slot(SlotStart, SlotEnd),
StartTime >= SlotStart,
EndTime = StartTime + Duration,
EndTime =< SlotEnd.
```

Financial Risk Assessment

This is where logic programming gets really interesting. Instead of solving a puzzle with a single solution, we're dealing with scenarios and probabilities. Think of it as playing thousands of "what-if" games simultaneously:

- "If interest rates rise by X

- "If market volatility exceeds Y

- "If currency exchange rates fluctuate within Z range..."

Just as we used logical rules to deduce who took the cookie, we can use similar principles to assess financial risks and make predictions.

A simplified risk assessment model:

```
% Facts: investment types and their risk factors
investment(stocks_tech, high_risk).
investment(govt_bonds, low_risk).
investment(real_estate, medium_risk).

risk_factor(high_risk, 0.8).
```

```
risk_factor(medium_risk, 0.5).
risk_factor(low_risk, 0.2).

market_condition(volatile).
interest_rate(low).

% Rules for risk assessment
risk_level(Investment, TotalRisk) :-
    investment(Investment, RiskType),
    risk_factor(RiskType, BaseFactor),
    market_multiplier(Multiplier),
    TotalRisk is BaseFactor * Multiplier.

% Market conditions affect risk
market_multiplier(1.5) :- market_condition(volatile).
market_multiplier(1.0) :- market_condition(stable).
```

Customer Service Routing

Remember how we matched teachers to classes based on their expertise and availability? Customer service routing follows a similar pattern. Instead of finding who teaches what, we're determining:

- Which agent is best suited for each customer query

- How to minimize wait times while maximizing satisfaction

- When to escalate issues to specialists

The logical approach helps create efficient, intelligent routing systems that adapt in real-time.

Here's how we might model customer service routing:

```prolog
% Facts: agents and their skills
agent(john, [technical, english, spanish]).
agent(mary, [billing, english, french]).
agent(steve, [technical, billing, english]).

% Current agent status
available(john).
available(mary).
busy(steve).

% Customer queries
query_type(ticket_1, technical).
query_type(ticket_2, billing).
language(ticket_1, spanish).
language(ticket_2, english).

% Rules for matching
can_handle(Agent, Ticket) :-
    agent(Agent, Skills),
    query_type(Ticket, QueryType),
    language(Ticket, Lang),
    member(QueryType, Skills),
    member(Lang, Skills),
    available(Agent).
```

Project Resource Management

This is like our class scheduling problem on steroids. Instead of just matching teachers to classrooms, we're juggling:

- Multiple projects with varying priorities

- Team members with different skills and availability

- Budget constraints and deadlines

- Equipment and facility usage

Logic programming helps find optimal allocations while respecting all these constraints – just as it helped us solve complex puzzles, but with real business impact.

A basic project resource allocation system:

```
% Facts: team members and their skills
employee(alice, [java, python, leadership]).
employee(bob, [python, database]).
employee(carol, [design, javascript]).

% Project tasks and requirements
task(backend_dev, [python, database], 20).    % 20 hours
task(frontend_dev, [javascript], 15).
task(team_lead, [leadership], 10).

% Resource availability (hours per week)
available_hours(alice, 30).
available_hours(bob, 25).
available_hours(carol, 35).

% Rules for assignment
can_assign(Employee, Task) :-
    employee(Employee, Skills),
    task(Task, Requirements, Hours),
    available_hours(Employee, Available),
    Available >= Hours,
```

```
all_skills_match(Requirements, Skills).

all_skills_match([], _).
all_skills_match([R|Rest], Skills) :-
    member(R, Skills),
    all_skills_match(Rest, Skills).
```

Benefits of Logic Programming in Business

Here's where we tie everything together. The benefits extend far beyond just solving complex problems:

• Maintenance and Adaptability: Just like how we could easily add new rules to our puzzles, businesses can quickly adapt their logic to changing conditions

• Transparency: The declarative nature means business rules are expressed clearly and explicitly

• Optimization: The ability to find optimal solutions among millions of possibilities

• Problem-solving approach: A natural way to express business rules and constraints

The real power isn't just in solving individual problems – it's in providing a different way of thinking about business challenges. Just as we approached our puzzles by stating what we know and what must be true, we can approach complex business problems with the same clarity and logical rigor.

This transition from puzzles to real-world business applications shows why logic programming isn't just an academic exercise – it's a powerful tool for tackling some of the most complex challenges in modern business operations.

A Natural Evolution

As we've seen, Prolog's approach to logical reasoning is powerful, but it has its limitations. While Prolog excels at deductive reasoning – drawing conclusions from known facts – real-world problems often require us to reason with incomplete information, explore multiple possible scenarios, or deal with conflicting rules. This is where Answer Set Programming (ASP) steps in.

Think of the transition from Prolog to ASP like moving from classical logic to human-like reasoning. In the real world, we often need to make assumptions, handle exceptions, and reason with "common sense." For instance, when planning a dinner, we naturally assume that if a recipe doesn't explicitly mention exotic ingredients, it probably uses common ones. This kind of default reasoning is awkward to express in Prolog but natural in ASP.

Let's look at a simple example that highlights the difference:

In Prolog, expressing"birds typically fly" is cumbersome:

```
flies(X) :- bird(X), \+ abnormal_bird(X).
abnormal_bird(penguin).
abnormal_bird(ostrich).
```

In ASP, we can write more naturally:

```
flies(X) :- bird(X), not -flies(X).
-flies(X) :- penguin(X).
bird(X) :- penguin(X).
bird(X) :- sparrow(X).
```

While this example might seem simple, it reveals a fundamental shift in thinking. ASP allows us to:

- Express defaults and exceptions naturally

- Handle conflicting rules elegantly

- Find multiple possible solutions (answer sets)

- Work with incomplete information

As we move into the next chapter, we'll explore how this different way of thinking – the "answer set mind" – opens up new possibilities for solving complex problems that were difficult or impossible with traditional logic programming.

Let's dive into the world of Answer Set Programming, where we'll discover how to think in terms of possible worlds and stable models, and see how this powerful paradigm tackles problems that challenge traditional approaches.

The Answer Set Mind

Have you ever noticed how humans naturally reason about everyday problems? We make assumptions, change our minds when new information arrives, and often think about what "could be" rather than just what "is." Traditional programming, even logic programming as we explored with Prolog, doesn't quite capture this natural way of thinking.

Enter Answer Set Programming (ASP) – a paradigm that feels remarkably close to human reasoning. If Prolog was about deducing facts from rules, ASP is about exploring possibilities and finding solutions that make sense given our constraints and preferences.

In this chapter, we'll discover a different way of thinking about problems. We'll learn how to express problems in terms of constraints and choices, see how ASP handles the kind of reasoning that comes naturally to us humans, and explore real-world applications where this approach shines.

We'll be using **Clingo**, a powerful ASP solver, for our examples. Don't worry if you've never used it before – we'll start from the basics and build up to solving complex problems. By the end of this chapter, you'll have a new tool in your programming toolbox, one that might just change how you think about problem-solving itself.

Let's begin by understanding what makes the"answer set mind" different from what we've seen before.

Thinking in Constraints and Possibilities

The Fundamental Shift

In our journey through logic programming, we've been thinking like Prolog: writing rules to deduce what's true, building proof trees, and following logical consequences. But take a moment and think about how you solve real-world problems. When you're planning a dinner party, do you build a proof tree? Of course not! You probably think more like:

"Let's see... I could make pasta, or maybe that new fish recipe. Wait, if I make fish, I'll need to get fresh ingredients. Oh, and Sarah can't eat dairy, so if she comes, the pasta's out..."

This natural way of reasoning – thinking about possibilities, constraints, and consequences – is exactly what Answer Set Programming (ASP) is designed for. Instead of telling the computer "how" to solve a problem step by step, we describe "what" makes a solution valid or invalid.

Answer Sets and Stable Models

In traditional programming, we typically get one answer – the output of our algorithm. Even in Prolog, we usually work toward finding a single solution through logical deduction. But human reasoning often explores multiple possibilities simultaneously. When planning a dinner, we naturally think about several valid combinations at once.

This is where ASP shines with its concept of "answer sets" or "stable models." Each answer set represents a complete, self-consistent world that satisfies all our rules and constraints. Think of it like parallel universes – each one is a valid way things could be.

Let's see this with a simple dinner planning example:

```
% Possible main dishes we could make
dish(pasta). dish(fish). dish(steak).

% We must choose exactly one main dish
1 { serve(X) : dish(X) } 1.

% We can serve either red or white wine
1 { wine(red); wine(white) } 1.

% Fish doesn't go well with red wine
:- serve(fish), wine(red).
```

When we run this program, ASP doesn't just find one solution – it finds all possible stable models:

- serve(pasta), wine(red)
- serve(pasta), wine(white)
- serve(fish), wine(white)
- serve(steak), wine(red)
- serve(steak), wine(white)

Each answer set is stable because:

- It's complete – decisions are made about both the dish and wine

- It's consistent – no rules or constraints are violated

- It's minimal – contains only what's necessary

This mirrors how we naturally reason: "If we serve fish, we must have white wine... but if we serve pasta, we could have either wine..." We're not following a fixed procedure but rather exploring a space of possibilities that satisfy our requirements.

Let's add one more constraint to see how it affects our solution space:

```
% We prefer red wine with steak
#minimize { 1,X : serve(steak), wine(white) }.

% Or alternatively, using a hard constraint if we want
    to enforce it:
:- serve(steak), wine(white).
```

Now some solutions become more preferred than others, just like in real-world decision making. This is another way ASP mirrors human reasoning – we don't just find valid solutions, we can express preferences among them.

ASP in Action: Human-Like Reasoning

Before diving into the specific syntax and rules of ASP (which we'll cover in detail in the next sections), let's preview how ASP can model complex, human-like reasoning. Don't worry if some of the notation looks unfamiliar – we'll explain all the syntax elements later. For now, focus on how naturally ASP captures the way humans think through problems.

Consider planning a dinner party. As humans, we typically reason through multiple aspects simultaneously: who to invite, what to cook, and how to ensure everyone's dietary needs are met. Here's how we can express this in ASP:

```
% People we might invite
person(alice). person(bob). person(charlie).
person(david). person(eve).

% Choose 3 people to invite
3 { invite(X) : person(X) } 3.

% Social dynamics: Alice and Bob don't get along
:- invite(alice), invite(bob).

% Dietary restrictions
vegetarian(alice).
lactose_intolerant(charlie).

% Menu planning with constraints
1 { main(pasta); main(steak); main(vegetable_curry) }
    1.

% Respect dietary restrictions
:- invite(X), vegetarian(X), main(steak).
:- invite(X), lactose_intolerant(X), main(pasta).
```

Each answer set from this program represents a complete, valid dinner party plan. For example:

- `invite(alice)`, `invite(charlie)`, `invite(david)`, `main(vegetable_curry)`

- `invite(bob)`, `invite(david)`, `invite(eve)`, `main(steak)`

Even in this simple preview, we can see how ASP naturally handles:

- Choices (who to invite, what to serve)

- Hard constraints (dietary restrictions, social conflicts)

- Multiple interacting decisions (menu must work for all invited guests)

This mirrors how humans naturally approach such problems – we don't follow a step-by-step procedure, but rather consider multiple constraints and possibilities simultaneously. In the following sections, we'll break down the syntax and concepts that make this kind of declarative problem-solving possible.

Non-monotonicity and Negation As Failure

ASP's power for human-like reasoning comes from two key features that mirror how we naturally think: non-monotonic reasoning and negation as failure. Let's explore these concepts with simple examples before seeing how they work together.

Non-monotonic Reasoning:

In everyday life, we often change our conclusions when we get new information. ASP can do the same:

```
% Initial knowledge
day(saturday).
sunny :- day(saturday), not rainy(saturday).
outdoor_party :- sunny, not cancelled(outdoor_party).

% Initially concludes; outdoor_party is possible

% New information arrives
rainy(saturday).
% Now outdoor_party is no longer concluded
```

This ability to withdraw conclusions when new information arrives is fundamentally different from classical logic, where new information can only add conclusions, never remove them.

Negation as Failure (NAF):

Consider how you reason about going to a store: "If I haven't heard they're closed, I'll assume they're open." ASP captures this common-sense reasoning using negation as failure:

```
% If we don't know something is unavailable, assume it
    's available
available(X) :- ingredient(X), not out_of_stock(X).

% If we don't know someone has dietary restrictions,
    assume they can eat anything
can_eat(Person, Dish) :- person(Person), dish(Dish),
```

```
not has_restriction(Person, Dish).
```

Two Types of "No"

ASP provides two different ways to express negation:

Classical Negation (-p): "We know this is false" Negation as Failure (not p): "We can't prove this is true" Here's a medical diagnosis example showing the difference:

```
% Facts about a patient
symptom(fever).
symptom(cough).
-symptom(rash). % We explicitly confirmed there is NO
    rash
% Classical negation: we KNOW it's false

% Diagnostic rules
possible_flu :- symptom(fever), symptom(cough),
not symptom(rash). % NAF: can't prove rash exists

definitely_not_measles :- -symptom(rash), % Classical:
    proven no rash
symptom(fever).
```

The difference matters:

- -symptom(rash) means "We've checked, there's definitely no rash"

- not symptom(rash) means "We haven't established that there is a rash"

Let's see how these concepts work together in a restaurant scenario:

```
% Restaurant scenario
cuisine(italian). cuisine(indian).
friend(alice). friend(bob). friend(charlie).

% Choose a cuisine
1 { choose(X) : cuisine(X) } 1.

% Known preferences
likes(alice, italian).
-likes(bob, indian). % Bob definitely dislikes Indian
    food

% Charlie is easy-going -- will come unless we know
    they dislike it
will_come(charlie) :- friend(charlie), choose(Cuisine)
    ,
not -likes(charlie, Cuisine).

% Others come if they explicitly like the cuisine
will_come(Person) :- friend(Person), choose(Cuisine),
likes(Person, Cuisine).

% Try to get at least 2 friends to come
:- #count{X : will_come(X)} < 2.
```

This example combines everything we've discussed:

• Multiple possible solutions

• Both types of negation

- Default reasoning with incomplete information

- Constraints on valid solutions

The power of ASP comes from its ability to represent both definite knowledge ("Bob dislikes Indian food") and reasonable assumptions based on incomplete information ("Charlie will probably come since we don't know they dislike the cuisine"). This matches how humans naturally reason about problems.

ASP Tutorial: Getting Started

This tutorial uses Clingo's syntax (part of the Potassco suite of ASP tools) to introduce ASP programming. While other ASP systems like DLV, WASP, or s(CASP) may have their own syntax variations and specific features, Clingo has become a de facto standard in the ASP community. Its syntax is clean, well-documented, and supports most modern ASP features. Once you understand Clingo's syntax and concepts, you can easily adapt to other ASP systems if needed.

Basic Syntax and Concepts

ASP programs are built from three fundamental elements: facts, rules, and constraints. Let's look at each one:

Facts

Facts are simple statements that are always true:

```
person(john). % John is a person
age(john, 25). % John is 25 years old
likes(john, pizza). % John likes pizza
```

Rules

Rules let us define new facts based on existing ones:

```
% If someone is a person and their age is >= 18, they'
```

```
re an adult
adult(X) :- person(X), age(X, Y), Y >= 18.

% If someone is an adult and a citizen, they can vote
can_vote(X) :- adult(X), citizen(X).
```

Constraints

Constraints tell us what's not allowed:

```
% Cannot be an adult if under 18
:- adult(X), age(X, Y), Y < 18.

% Cannot be in two places at once
:- location(Person, Place1), location(Person, Place2),
     Place1 != Place2.
```

Important syntax rules:

- Variables start with uppercase (X, Y)

- Constants start with lowercase (john, pizza)

- Each statement ends with a period

- Comments start with

Making Choices

Choice rules allow ASP to select from multiple possibilities. Let's understand their syntax:

```
% Available colors
color(red). color(blue). color(green).

% Basic choice rule syntax:
L { head_predicate : range_predicate } U

% Where:
% L = lower bound (minimum number to choose)
% U = upper bound (maximum number to choose)
% head_predicate = what we're creating
% range_predicate = what we're choosing from

% Example: Assign exactly one color to each node
1 { color(Node, C) : color(C) } 1 :- node(Node).
% This means:
% - Left 1 = must choose at least 1 color
% - Right 1 = must choose at most 1 color
% - Together: must choose exactly 1 color
% - For each Node, create color(Node, C) by selecting
%   from available color(C)

% More choice patterns with bounds:
{ selected(X) : item(X) } 3.
% No lower bound (0), upper bound 3
% Meaning: Select anywhere from 0 to 3 items

2 { selected(X) : item(X) }.
% Lower bound 2, no upper bound
% Meaning: Select 2 or more items

2 { selected(X) : item(X) } 4.
% Lower bound 2, upper bound 4
% Meaning: Select between 2 and 4 items
```

When reading a choice rule:

- If only one number is present with no right bound: it's a lower bound

- If only one number is present with no left bound: it's an upper bound

- If both numbers are the same: it means "exactly this many"

- If no numbers are present: it means "any number" (0 or more)

Useful Built-in Features

ASP provides several built-in features that make common programming tasks easier. Let's explore the most frequently used ones:

Number Ranges and Comparisons

The range syntax (. .) is a convenient way to generate sequences of numbers. Comparison operators help express numerical relationships:

```
% Number ranges
number(1..10).  % Creates facts: number(1), number(2),
      ..., number(10)

% Comparison operators
```

```
X != Y % Not equal
X < Y % Less than
X <= Y % Less than or equal
X > Y % Greater than
X >= Y % Greater than or equal

% Example using ranges and comparisons
valid_age(X) :- number(X), X >= 0, X <= 120.
```

Aggregates

Aggregates are powerful features that perform calculations over sets of values. The most common aggregates are:

```
% #count: counts the number of elements
total_students(C) :- C = #count{ X : student(X) }.
% Counts how many X satisfy student(X)

% #sum: adds up values
total_cost(S) :- S = #sum{ C,I : item(I), cost(I,C) }.
% Sums all costs C for each item I

% #max and #min: find extreme values
highest_grade(M) :- M = #max{ G : grade(_,G) }.
lowest_grade(M) :- M = #min{ G : grade(_,G) }.
% Finds the highest/lowest grade G among all grades
```

The underscore (_) in grade(_,G) is a placeholder variable when we don't need to use that value.

Common Aggregate Patterns

Here are some typical use cases for aggregates:

```
% Count items meeting a condition
expensive_items(N) :- N = #count{ I : item(I), cost(I,
    C), C > 100 }.

% Calculate average (using sum and count)
average_grade(A) :- total(S), count(C), A = S/C,
    total(S) :- S = #sum{ G : grade(,G) },
    count(C) :- C = #count{ G : grade(,G) }.

% Find items with maximum value
best_item(I) :-
item(I), value(I,V),
V = #max{ V1 : item(I1), value(I1,V1) }.
```

These built-in features make ASP particularly powerful for solving complex problems involving counting, summing, or finding optimal values. When combined with choice rules and constraints, they allow you to express sophisticated requirements in a concise way.

Your First ASP Program: A Simple Meal Planner

Let's build a weekly meal planner step by step:

```
% Step 1: Define our menu
dish(pasta). dish(salad). dish(soup).
dish(steak). dish(fish).
```

```
% Step 2: Add dish properties
vegetarian(pasta). vegetarian(salad). vegetarian(soup)
   .
high_protein(steak). high_protein(fish).

% Step 3: Define the days
day(1..7). % Creates days 1 through 7

% Step 4: Choose one meal per day
1 { meal(Day,D) : dish(D) } 1 :- day(Day).

% Step 5: Add constraints
% No same dish on consecutive days
:- meal(D1,X), meal(D2,X), D2 = D1 + 1.

% No high-protein dishes on consecutive days
:- meal(D,X), high_protein(X),
meal(D+1,Y), high_protein(Y).

% Show only the meal assignments
#show meal/2.
```

To run this program using Clingo:

```
% Find one solution
clingo mealplan.lp

% Find 10 different solutions
clingo mealplan.lp -n 10

% Find all possible solutions
clingo mealplan.lp -n 0
```

You'll get solutions like:

```
Answer: 1
meal(1,pasta) meal(2,fish) meal(3,salad)
meal(4,steak) meal(5,soup) meal(6,pasta) meal(7,fish)
```

Each solution represents a valid meal plan where:

- Every day has exactly one meal

- No meal repeats on consecutive days

- High-protein meals (steak and fish) aren't served back-to-back

How ASP Solves Complex Puzzles

Remember when we were kids, solving puzzles like finding our way through a maze or fitting shapes together? ASP approaches puzzles in a fascinating way that's quite different from how we humans typically solve them. Instead of trying one solution at a time like we do, ASP considers all possible solutions at once and then filters out the ones that don't work.

In this section, we'll explore how ASP tackles puzzles and what makes its approach special. We'll look at common patterns that show up in puzzle solving, learn some clever tricks to make our solutions more efficient, and see how to build our solutions step by step. Whether you're interested in solving Sudoku, planning optimal routes, or tackling other complex problems, understanding these concepts will help you write better ASP programs.

Difference From Prolog's Approach

Let's talk about what makes ASP special compared to Prolog. While both are logic programming languages, they think about problems in very different ways:

- Prolog works like a detective, starting with what it wants to prove and working backwards to find evidence. It's systematic but can get stuck in endless searches.

- ASP is more like a creative thinker – it imagines all possible scenarios that could work, then filters out the ones that don't fit our rules. It's great at finding solutions when we don't know how to start searching.

Let's see this difference with a simple example – finding a path between two points:

```
% Prolog approach (procedural):
path(X,Y) :- connected(X,Y).
path(X,Y) :- connected(X,Z), path(Z,Y).
?- path(start, end). % Query that triggers backward
    search

% ASP approach (declarative):
{ selected(X,Y) } :- connected(X,Y). % Generate
    possible paths
:- selected(X,Y), selected(Y,Z), not selected(X,Z). %
    Must be transitive
:- not reach(end). % Must reach the end
reach(Y) :- selected(X,Y), reach(X). % Define
    reachability
reach(start). % Starting point
```

This difference becomes even clearer in more complex puzzles. Take the famous 8-Queens problem (placing 8 queens on a chess board so none can attack each other):

- Prolog would try to place queens one by one, backtracking when it hits conflicts – like a person solving the puzzle

- ASP takes a different approach: it imagines all possible queen arrangements at once, then removes the invalid ones – more like having a magical vision of all possibilities

Here's how we'd write the 8-Queens in ASP:

```
% ASP Solution for 8-Queens
#const n = 8.
row(1..n). col(1..n).

% Generate: Place queens (imagine all possibilities)
1 { queen(R,C) : col(C) } 1 :- row(R).

% Test: Remove invalid arrangements
:- queen(R1,C1), queen(R2,C2), R1 != R2, C1 = C2. %
    Same column
:- queen(R1,C1), queen(R2,C2), |R1-R2| = |C1-C2|. %
    Diagonal
```

Common Patterns in Puzzle Solving

When you solve enough puzzles with ASP, you start to see some common patterns. Let's look at the most useful ones:

Generate and Test Pattern

This is the bread and butter of ASP puzzle solving. Think of it like a two-step process:

- First, we generate all possible solutions (the "what if" phase)

- Then, we test and remove the invalid ones (the "reality check" phase)

Here's a simple example – coloring a map so no adjacent regions have the same color:

```
% Given: regions and their neighbors
region(1..4).
neighbor(1,2). neighbor(2,3). neighbor(3,4). neighbor
    (4,1).
color(red;blue;green).

% Generate: Give each region one color
1 { colored(Region,Color) : color(Color) } 1 :- region
    (Region).

% Test: No neighbors share colors
:- neighbor(X,Y), colored(X,C), colored(Y,C).
```

Symmetry Breaking

Many puzzles have multiple solutions that are basically mirror images of each other. We can help ASP work faster by telling it to ignore these duplicates. It's like telling someone solving a puzzle "don't bother trying the same thing upside down":

```
% Example with bin packing
item(1..5). bin(1..3).

% Generate: Place items in bins
1 { in_bin(I,B) : bin(B) } 1 :- item(I).

% Symmetry breaking: First item must go in first bin
:- item(1), in_bin(1,B), B > 1.

% Keep bins in order (another symmetry break)
```

```
:- in_bin(I1,B1), in_bin(I2,B2),
I1 < I2, B1 > B2,
#min{ I : in_bin(I,B1) } = I1,
#min{ I : in_bin(I,B2) } = I2.
```

Constraint Encoding

Writing good constraints is an art. We can write them in different ways:

- Direct constraints – explicitly saying what's not allowed

- Implied constraints – adding extra rules that must be true

Here's how this looks in Sudoku:

```
% Direct constraint: No repeated numbers in a row
:- cell(X,Y1,N), cell(X,Y2,N), Y1 != Y2.

% Implied constraint: Every row must sum to 45
sum_row(R,S) :- R = #sum{ V,C : cell(R,C,V) }.
:- sum_row(R,S), S != 45.
```

Step-by-step Solution Development

When you're writing an ASP solution, it's best to build it up gradually, like constructing a building. Remember our Sudoku solver in Prolog from the previous chapter? The one with all those complex predicates for checking rows, columns, and boxes? Well, you're in for a treat – the ASP version is surprisingly concise. This really shows how ASP's declarative nature can simplify complex problems.

Here's the process I usually follow:

- Define what's possible (the building blocks)

- Add basic rules for generating solutions

- Start with the simplest constraints

- Add more complex constraints

- Add optimization if needed

Let's see this in action with a complete Sudoku solver:

```
% 1. Define what's possible
dim(1..9).
box_dim(1..3).

% 2. Basic rules: each cell needs exactly one number
1 { cell(X,Y,N) : dim(N) } 1 :- dim(X), dim(Y).

% 3. Simple constraints
% Each row must have distinct numbers
:- cell(X,Y1,N), cell(X,Y2,N), Y1 != Y2.

% Each column must have distinct numbers
:- cell(X1,Y,N), cell(X2,Y,N), X1 != X2.

% 4. More complex constraint: boxes must have distinct
%    numbers
box_id(X,Y,B) :- dim(X), dim(Y), B = ((X-1)/3)*3 + ((Y
    -1)/3) + 1.
```

```
:- cell(X1,Y1,N), cell(X2,Y2,N), box_id(X1,Y1,B),
   box_id(X2,Y2,B), (X1,Y1) != (X2,Y2).

% 5. Add initial values (if any)
% Example: cell(1,1,5). cell(1,2,3). etc.
```

Compare this with our Prolog version – no need for complex recursion or backtracking predicates! ASP handles all that automatically. We just need to state what makes a valid solution, and ASP figures out how to find it.

Optimization in Puzzle Solving

Sometimes finding any solution isn't enough – we want the best solution. ASP can help us here too! While Prolog would need complex recursive predicates with careful tracking of costs, ASP handles optimization elegantly with built-in minimize and maximize statements.

Let's look at a practical example – finding the shortest path in a grid. Think of this like a robot trying to navigate from one corner of a room to another, always looking for the shortest route.

Here's what makes this interesting:

- First, we need to find a valid path (any path will do)

- Then, among all valid paths, we want the shortest one

- ASP will handle both tasks for us automatically

Here's how we write it:

```
% Define our grid
point(1..5,1..5).
% Where we can move
move(X,Y,NX,NY) :- point(X,Y), point(NX,NY), |X-NX| +
    |Y-NY| = 1.

% Start and finish points
start(1,1). end(5,5).

% Generate possible paths
{ path(X,Y,NX,NY) } :- move(X,Y,NX,NY).

% Make sure we can reach the end
reached(X,Y) :- start(X,Y).
reached(NX,NY) :- reached(X,Y), path(X,Y,NX,NY).
:- not reached(EX,EY), end(EX,EY).

% Count our steps
steps(N) :- N = #count{ X,Y,NX,NY : path(X,Y,NX,NY) }.

% Find the shortest path
#minimize { N : steps(N) }.
```

Notice how natural this feels – we just tell ASP to minimize the number of steps, and it handles all the complex optimization logic for us. We could easily modify this to handle different scenarios:

- Finding paths that avoid certain areas (just add constraints)

- Minimizing total distance instead of steps (change what we're counting)

- Finding paths that balance length against other factors (use weighted optimization)

This optimization capability makes ASP particularly powerful for real-world problems where we're not just looking for any solution, but the best one according to some criteria.

Handling Combinatorial Problems Efficiently

Sometimes our puzzles get really big, and ASP might struggle to solve them quickly. Here are some tricks I've learned to help with this:

Reduce the Search Space

Think about a maze – it's easier to solve if you can eliminate dead ends before you start. Same idea in ASP:

```
% Instead of this (too many possibilities):
position(1..64). % chess board
{ piece(P,X) : position(X) }.

% Do this (more focused):
valid_position(1..8). % only first rank
{ piece(P,X) : valid_position(X) }.
```

Use Time Steps Wisely

When your puzzle involves sequences of moves, be clear about time steps:

```
% Better approach -- clear time boundaries
step(1..maxsteps).
move(X,Y,S) :- position(X;Y), step(S).
```

Break Down Complex Problems

Sometimes it's better to solve a problem in pieces. Think of it like eating an elephant – one bite at a time:

```
% Stage 1: Find valid positions
valid_pos(X,Y) :- in_bounds(X,Y), not blocked(X,Y).

% Stage 2: Find possible moves between positions
can_move(X1,Y1,X2,Y2) :- valid_pos(X1,Y1), valid_pos(
    X2,Y2),
|X1-X2| + |Y1-Y2| = 1.
```

Remember, these are guidelines, not strict rules. Every puzzle is different, and part of the fun is figuring out which approaches work best for your specific problem. The key is to start simple and build up to more complex solutions as needed.

Modeling Real-world Problems

So far, we've looked at clean, well-defined puzzles. But real life is messier! Let's see how ASP can tackle real-world problems through some practical examples.

From Business Rules to ASP Code

Imagine you're helping a small café manager create their weekly staff schedule. They tell you:

"I need at least two people per shift, nobody should work more than 40 hours a week, and please, no one should work two night shifts in a row – it's too tiring!"

How do we turn these natural requirements into ASP? Let's break it down:

```
employee(alice; bob; charlie; diana).
shift(morning; afternoon; night).
day(1..7).

% First, let's generate possible schedules
{ works(E,S,D) : shift(S) } 1 :- employee(E), day(D).

% Now for the manager's rules:
% "At least two people per shift"
:- shift(S), day(D),
   #count { E : works(E,S,D) } < 2.

% "No more than 40 hours per week"
```

```
:- employee(E),
   #count { S,D : works(E,S,D) } * 8 > 40.

% "No consecutive night shifts"
:- works(E,night,D), works(E,night,D+1),
   day(D), day(D+1).
```

See how each business rule becomes a constraint? It's like translating from English to ASP!

Dealing With Uncertainty

Real life isn't just about rules – it's also about dealing with unknowns. Let's say you're planning a construction project, but you're not sure if it will rain tomorrow. Here's how ASP can help:

```
day(1..5).    % 5-day project
task(foundation; walls; roof).

% We don't know which days will rain
{ rainy(D) } :- day(D).

% Can't do outdoor work in rain
:- schedule(Task,D), outdoor_task(Task), rainy(D).
```

Let's break down what this code means. The line rainy(D) is telling ASP "I don't know if it will rain or not – consider both possibilities." It's like saying "each day could be rainy or sunny, please figure out plans for all cases."

So when ASP runs this program, it will:

1. Consider some days might be rainy, some not

2. Generate different possible schedules

3. Make sure no outdoor work is scheduled on rainy days

It's like when you're planning a picnic and you say "Well, if it rains on Saturday, we'll do it on Sunday instead." ASP automatically considers all these "what-if" scenarios and finds solutions that work in each case.

This is much more realistic than assuming perfect knowledge. In real life, we often have to make plans while dealing with uncertainties – will it rain? Will everyone show up? Will the delivery arrive on time? ASP helps us create flexible plans that can handle these uncertainties.

Making Trade-offs

In real life, we rarely have perfect solutions. Instead, we're constantly balancing different goals. Let's look at a real example: planning a road trip.

Imagine you're planning a drive from New York to Boston. You might care about several things:

- How long will it take? (shortest route)

- How much will it cost? (avoiding toll roads)

- How enjoyable is the drive? (scenic routes)

ASP can help find the sweet spot:

```
route_option(highway; scenic; backroad).
point(nyc; hartford; boston).

% This line means "for each pair of points, pick one
    type of route"
{ take_route(From,To,Type) : route_option(Type) } 1 :-
    point(From), point(To), From != To.

% Define the characteristics of each route type
time(highway, nyc, hartford, 2).      % 2 hours
time(scenic, nyc, hartford, 3).       % 3 hours
time(backroad, nyc, hartford, 4).     % 4 hours

toll_cost(highway, nyc, hartford, 30).   % $30
toll_cost(scenic, nyc, hartford, 10).    % $10
toll_cost(backroad, nyc, hartford, 0).   % free

% Balance different factors -- like juggling multiple
    priorities
#minimize {
    Hours*2, R : time(R,_,_,Hours);       % Time is
        very important
    Cost, R    : toll_cost(R,_,_,Cost)    % Cost is
        less important
}.
```

The #minimize statement is like telling ASP "find me a route that's mostly quick, but also try to keep the costs down if you can." The *2 after Hours means we care twice as much about saving time as we do about saving money.

It's like when you're grocery shopping – you might prefer

organic produce, but not if it's three times the price. Or when choosing a restaurant – you want good food, but also consider the distance and price. ASP helps balance these competing goals to find the best overall solution.

Think about your own decision-making. What factors do you balance when choosing where to live, which job to take, or even what to eat for dinner? How would you express these trade-offs to ASP?

A Word About Testing

Let me share a small story. When I first started using ASP to help a local restaurant with their staff scheduling, I created this complex program with all sorts of fancy rules:

```
% Complex version -- too much at once!
employee(zhang;wang;li;chen;park;singh).
shift(morning;afternoon;evening).
day(monday;tuesday;wednesday;thursday;friday;saturday;
    sunday).
skill(cooking;serving;cleaning).
language(chinese;english;korean).

% Generate schedules
{ works(E,S,D) : shift(S) } 1 :- employee(E), day(D).

% Every shift needs specific skills
has_skill(zhang,cooking). has_skill(wang,serving).
has_skill(li,cleaning). has_skill(chen,cooking).
required_skill(morning,cooking,2). required_skill(
    morning,serving,1).
```

```
:- shift(S), day(D), skill(SK),
required_skill(S,SK,N),
#count { E : works(E,S,D), has_skill(E,SK) } < N.

% Language requirements
speaks(zhang,chinese). speaks(wang,chinese). speaks(
    chen,korean).
:- shift(S), day(D),
not #count { E : works(E,S,D), speaks(E,chinese) } >=
    1.

% Break requirements
:- works(E,S1,D), works(E,S2,D2),
S1 != S2, D2 = D + 1,
shift_end(S1,T1), shift_start(S2,T2),
T2 - T1 < 8.

% And many more complex rules...
```

But when we tried to use it, nothing worked! Can you guess what I learned? I should have tested it with a tiny example first.

Here's the simple approach I wish I'd started with:

```
% Start with just two employees and two shifts
test_employee(zhang; wang).
test_shift(morning; afternoon).
test_day(monday; tuesday).

% Try the basic scheduling rule
{ works(E,S,D) : test_shift(S) } 1 :-
    test_employee(E), test_day(D).

% Test one simple rule first
```

```
:- test_shift(S), test_day(D),
   #count { E : works(E,S,D) } < 1.
```

It's like learning to cook – you don't start by making a five-course meal. You start with something simple, like boiling an egg. Once that works, you gradually add more ingredients and techniques.

Here's my practical advice for testing your ASP programs:

1. Start tiny – use just 2-3 items for each type of thing

2. Test one rule at a time

3. When something doesn't work, you'll find the problem much faster

4. Only add more complexity when the simple version works

Remember: your ASP program doesn't need to handle every possible case right away. It's okay to start small and grow your solution step by step. That's how we solve real problems in the real world!

Success Stories: ASP in Action

Let's look at some typical scenarios where ASP shines in real-world applications. These examples will show you how ASP solves problems you might encounter in your own work.

Production Scheduling

Imagine a factory that paints cars. It's not as simple as just painting them in order – here's why:

- Each color change wastes paint and time (up to 50 liters per change!)

- Some orders are urgent (premium customers need priority)

- Machines need maintenance (every 8 hours of operation)

- Workers have shift changes (three shifts per day)

- Some colors need longer drying times

Here's how ASP can handle this kind of scheduling:

```
car(1..20). % today's production
color(red; blue; white; black).
time_slot(1..30).
priority_car(5;12;18). % urgent orders

% Each car needs painting
1 { schedule(Car,Time,Color) : time_slot(Time), color(
    Color) } 1 :- car(Car).
```

```
% Minimize color changes
color_change(T) :- schedule(C1,T,Color1), schedule(C2,
    T+1,Color2), Color1 != Color2.

% Priority cars must be done in first 10 slots
:- priority_car(C), schedule(C,T,_), T > 10.

% Maintenance breaks
maintenance(T) :- T mod 8 = 0.
:- schedule(,T,), maintenance(T).

#minimize { 1@2,T : color_change(T) }.
#minimize { T@1,C : schedule(C,T,_), priority_car(C)
    }.
```

This program not only groups similar colors but also handles priorities and maintenance. Using this type of optimization can help factories significantly reduce paint waste and improve efficiency!

Network Security

Think about protecting a computer network. You need to:

- Watch for suspicious activity

- Cover all important connections

- Stay within your budget (monitors cost $5000 each)

- Adapt when the network changes

- Consider different security levels

Here's a more detailed ASP approach:

```
node(server; desktop1; desktop2; wifi_router).
link(server,desktop1). link(server,desktop2).
link(wifi_router,desktop1).
importance(server,3). importance(wifi_router,2).
importance(desktop1,1). importance(desktop2,1).

% Place security monitors
{ monitor(N) } :- node(N).

% Every link must be watched
watched(N1,N2) :- link(N1,N2), monitor(N1).
watched(N1,N2) :- link(N1,N2), monitor(N2).
:- link(N1,N2), not watched(N1,N2).

% High importance nodes need direct monitoring
:- importance(N,Level), Level > 2, not monitor(N).

% Budget constraint (maximum 3 monitors)
:- #count{ N : monitor(N) } > 3.

% Minimize costs while maximizing coverage
#minimize { 1@2,N : monitor(N) }.
#maximize { Level@1,N : importance(N,Level), monitor(N
    ) }.
```

Using this type of approach, companies can significantly reduce their monitoring costs while maintaining or even improving their security coverage!

Product Configuration

Consider configuring smartphones. You have:

- Different components (screens, batteries, cameras, processors)

- Complex compatibility rules

- Various price points (200−1000 range)

- Regional requirements (like network bands)

- Power and thermal constraints

Here's a more realistic ASP configuration:

```
part(screen_hd; screen_4k; battery_small;
    battery_large).
feature(5g; waterproof; fast_charge).
price(screen_hd,100). price(screen_4k,200).
price(battery_small,50). price(battery_large,100).
power(screen_hd,2). power(screen_4k,4).
power(battery_small,0). power(battery_large,0).

% Build valid combinations
{ use(P) : part(P) }.
{ has(F) : feature(F) }.

% Technical constraints
:- use(screen_4k), not use(battery_large).
:- has(fast_charge), not use(battery_large).

% Power budget
```

```
total_power(P) :- P = #sum{ W,Part : use(Part), power(
    Part,W) }.
:- total_power(P), P > 5.

% Price constraints
total_cost(C) :- C = #sum{ Price,Part : use(part(Part)
    ), price(Part,Price) }.
:- total_cost(C), C > 400. % budget model constraint

% Regional requirements
:- region(asia), has(5g), not has(waterproof). %
    market preference
```

This type of configuration system could help manufacturers dramatically reduce their product validation time, potentially turning weeks of work into a much faster automated process!

The Common Thread

What makes these success stories interesting isn't just the solutions themselves, but how ASP handles complexity in a natural way:

- Rules can be added incrementally as requirements change

- The same program works for different sizes of problems

- Optimization happens automatically

- Solutions are guaranteed to meet all constraints

The real power comes from ASP's ability to handle these

complex, interconnected rules while finding optimal solutions. Whether you're dealing with scheduling, configuration, or any problem with multiple competing requirements, ASP provides a natural way to express and solve them.

In practice, these examples often combine and overlap. A manufacturing plant might need to handle scheduling AND configuration AND security. ASP's modularity makes it easy to combine these different aspects into a single, coherent solution.

What's particularly exciting is seeing these techniques applied to new domains. From urban planning to curriculum design, people are discovering that many real-world problems share these same underlying patterns that ASP handles so well.

Advanced Concepts and Best Practices

Let's talk about taking your ASP skills to the next level. These practices come from solving real-world problems and will help you write more effective programs.

Making ASP Play Nice with Other Systems

ASP is powerful, but it really shines when integrated with other tools. Here's a practical approach to integration:

```python
from clingo import Control, Symbol
import json

class ScheduleSolver:
    def __init__(self):
        self.ctl = Control()
        self.ctl.load("schedule.lp")

    def add_employees(self, employees):
        # Add facts from external data
        for emp in employees:
            self.ctl.add("base", [], f"employee({emp})
                .")
            if emp.get('preferences'):
                for pref in emp['preferences']:
                    self.ctl.add("base", [],
                        f"prefers({emp['id']},{pref}).
                        ")

    def solve(self):
```

```python
        self.ctl.ground([("base", [])])
        solutions = []
        for answer in self.ctl.solve(yield_=True):
            # Convert to useful format
            solution = {
                'assignments': self._parse_assignments
                    (answer)
            }
            solutions.append(solution)
        return solutions

    def _parse_assignments(self, answer):
        assignments = {}
        for atom in answer.symbols(shown=True):
            if atom.name == "works":
                emp, shift = atom.arguments
                assignments[str(emp)] = str(shift)
        return assignments

# Usage example
solver = ScheduleSolver()
employees = [
    {'id': 'alice', 'preferences': ['morning']},
    {'id': 'bob', 'preferences': ['evening']}
]
solver.add_employees(employees)
result = solver.solve()
```

This approach shows how to:

- Create a reusable solver class

- Handle structured data input

- Convert ASP solutions to useful formats

- Maintain clean separation of concerns

Making Programs Faster

Performance optimization in ASP requires understanding how the solver works. Here are key techniques:

```
% Bad: Generating huge search space
time(1..1000).
{ schedule(Task,T) : time(T) }.

% Better: Smart domain restriction
time(1..1000).
task_duration(task1,5). task_duration(task2,3).
valid_start(Task,T) :- time(T), task_duration(Task,D),
    T + D <= 1000.

% Only generate possible assignments
{ start(Task,T) : valid_start(Task,T) } 1 :- task(Task
    ).

% Use helper predicates for complex conditions
ends_at(Task,End) :- start(Task,T), task_duration(Task
    ,D), End = T + D.

% Efficient overlap checking
:- start(Task1,T1), start(Task2,T2),
   ends_at(Task1,E1), ends_at(Task2,E2),
   Task1 != Task2,
   T1 <= T2, T2 < E1.
```

Key optimization principles:

- Restrict domains early

- Use helper predicates for reused calculations

- Structure constraints to minimize grounding

- Consider symmetry breaking when appropriate

Writing Clear Programs

Clear ASP programs follow a logical structure and use consistent naming:

```
%%% Domain Definition %%%
employee(alice;bob;charlie).
shift(morning;evening).
skill_level(junior;senior).

%%% Employee Properties %%%
has_skill(alice,senior). has_skill(bob,junior).
prefers_shift(alice,morning).
requires_supervision(E) :- has_skill(E,junior).

%%% Assignment Rules %%%
% Each employee gets exactly one shift
1 { works(E,S) : shift(S) } 1 :- employee(E).

%%% Business Constraints %%%
% Senior supervision required
has_senior(S) :- works(E,S), has_skill(E,senior).
:- works(E,S), requires_supervision(E), not has_senior
    (S).
```

```
%%% Optimization Goals %%%
#minimize { 1,E,S : works(E,S), not prefers_shift(E,S)
     }.

%%% Output Directives %%%
#show works/2.
```

Organization principles:

- Group related rules with clear comments

- Use consistent naming patterns

- Progress from simple to complex rules

- Separate generation from constraints

Avoiding Common Mistakes

Here are typical pitfalls and their solutions:

```
%%% Problem 1: Unbound Variables %%%
% Bad: Implicit domains
bad_rule(X) :- value(X), X < 10.

% Good: Explicit domains
number(1..9).
good_rule(X) :- number(X), value(X).

%%% Problem 2: Inefficient Counting %%%
% Bad: Repeated counting
:- #count { E : works(E,S) } > 3, shift(S).
```

```
% Good: Calculate once
shift_count(S,C) :- shift(S),
    C = #count { E : works(E,S) }.
:- shift_count(S,C), C > 3.

%%% Problem 3: Unnecessary Generation %%%
% Bad: Generate-then-filter
{ assign(Task,Resource) : resource(Resource) }.
:- assign(Task,Resource), not compatible(Task,Resource
    ).

% Good: Generate only valid options
{ assign(Task,Resource) : compatible(Task,Resource) }.
```

When Things Go Wrong

Systematic debugging in ASP:

```
%%% Debug Predicates %%%
% Track assignments
debug_assigned(E) :- works(E,_).
debug_unassigned(E) :- employee(E), not debug_assigned
    (E).

% Track constraint violations
violation(supervision,S) :- works(E,S),
    requires_supervision(E), not has_senior(S).

% Count important properties
count_assignments(C) :- C = #count { E,S : works(E,S)
    }.
```

```
count_violations(Type,C) :-
    C = #count { X : violation(Type,X) }.

%%% Debug Output %%%
#show debug_assigned/1.
#show debug_unassigned/1.
#show violation/2.
#show count_assignments/1.
#show count_violations/2.
```

Debugging strategy:

- Add counters for key properties

- Track constraint violations

- Use intermediate predicates

- Check small examples first

- Gradually add complexity

These practices help build robust, maintainable ASP solutions. Remember that clarity and correctness should come before optimization – make it work, then make it fast.

Now that you're familiar with functional programming, logic programming, and ASP, you might be wondering: "Which approach should I use for my specific problem?" In the next chapter, we'll tackle this question head-on, exploring how to choose the right paradigm and, sometimes more importantly, how to combine them effectively.

The Declarative Toolbox

Now that we've talked about functional programming, logic programming, and answer set programming, each of these approaches has its own special magic. But here's the real question: how do we choose which wand to wave for our specific problem? And can we sometimes use multiple wands together?

In this chapter, we'll explore exactly that. Think of it as your practical guide to the declarative world – not just theory, but real-world applications. We'll look at how to choose the right tool, mix different approaches, and learn from real industry experiences. By the end of this chapter, you'll have a clear framework for making these decisions in your own projects.

Understanding Your Problem Domain

Before we dive into choosing specific paradigms, let's talk about how to analyze your problem. It's like being a detective – you need to gather all the clues before you can solve the mystery. This crucial first step will make your paradigm choice much clearer and help you avoid the dreaded "solution in search of a problem" trap.

Identifying Problem Characteristics

Imagine you're examining your problem under a microscope. What do you see? Here are the key aspects to look for:

Data Flow Patterns

Think about how information moves through your system:

- Is it like a river, flowing in one direction? (streaming data)

- Or more like a lake, with data that needs to be stored and accessed? (state management)

- Maybe it's like a network of streams, with data merging and splitting? (parallel processing)

For example, in a video processing application, you have a clear stream: video frames flow in, get processed, and flow out. But in a banking system, you're dealing with more of a lake, where transaction history needs to be maintained and accessed.

State and Mutability

How much state does your system need to remember?

- Is it mostly about transforming input into output?
- Do you need to track history or maintain complex state?
- How important is data immutability?

Consider a weather forecasting system: while it processes huge amounts of data, each calculation is mainly about transforming current conditions into predictions. Contrast this with a game engine, which needs to maintain complex state about every object in the game world.

Constraint Landscapes

What rules and limitations shape your solution space?

- Business rules (like "no overdrafts allowed")
- Physical constraints (like "a robot can't be in two places at once")
- Resource limitations (like memory or processing power)
- Time constraints (real-time requirements)

Common Problem Patterns

Let's look at patterns that tend to point toward specific paradigms. Think of these as signposts helping you choose your path.

Data Transformation Patterns

These problems scream for functional programming:

Stream Processing:

- IoT sensor networks tracking environmental conditions

- Social media sentiment analysis in real-time

- Network packet inspection and filtering

- Financial market data processing

Here's a real example: A smart agriculture system processing data from thousands of soil sensors. Each reading goes through a pipeline of transformations:

1. Raw data cleanup

2. Unit conversion

3. Anomaly detection

4. Aggregation for analysis

Parallel Processing:

- Image processing (each pixel independently)

- Scientific simulations

- Batch data processing

Relationship and Rule Patterns

These are logic programming's sweet spot:

Knowledge Systems:

- Medical diagnosis systems connecting symptoms to conditions

- Legal expert systems navigating complex regulations

- Genetic relationship analysis

- Natural language understanding

Let's look at a fascinating example: A bioinformatics system analyzing gene interactions. It needs to:

- Understand relationships between genes

- Apply complex rules about gene expression

- Find patterns in genetic sequences

- Make predictions about protein interactions

Optimization and Planning Patterns

Answer Set Programming shines here:

Resource Allocation:

- University course scheduling

- Factory production line optimization

- Cloud resource management

- Sports league scheduling

Consider a modern pharmaceutical supply chain: You need to:

- Optimize manufacturing schedules

- Plan distribution routes

- Manage inventory levels

- Handle temperature-sensitive products

- Deal with varying lead times

Analyzing Requirements

Now, let's dig deeper into the practical considerations that will shape your choice.

Performance Requirements

Think about your system's need for speed:

Latency Considerations:

- Real-time systems (like trading platforms) need predictable, fast responses

- Batch processing systems can trade speed for thoroughness

- Interactive systems need to balance user experience with processing time

Scale Considerations:

- Data volume: Are we talking gigabytes or petabytes?

- Processing patterns: Burst or steady stream?

- Growth projections: How will needs change over time?

Maintenance and Evolution

Think about the future:

Code Maintenance:

- Who will maintain this code in six months?

- How easily can new team members understand it?

- How well does it document itself?

Requirement Changes:

- How likely are the requirements to change?

- What kinds of changes are expected?

- How easily can the system adapt?

Integration Requirements

Consider your system's neighborhood:

System Interactions:

- What existing systems must you work with?

- What APIs need to be supported?

- What data formats are involved?

Environmental Constraints:

- Available computing resources

- Network conditions

- Security requirements

- Compliance needs

Choosing the Right Paradigm

Now that we've dissected our problem, let's explore how to match it with the right paradigm. Remember, this isn't about finding a "perfect" solution – it's about finding the most effective approach for your specific situation.

When to Choose Functional Programming

Functional programming shines brightest in certain scenarios. Let's explore when it's your best bet.

Ideal Scenarios

Functional programming is particularly powerful when:

Data Transformation is Key:

- Processing streams of data

- Building data processing pipelines

- Implementing mathematical algorithms

- Handling concurrent operations

Example: Financial Data Processing Consider a real-time trading system:

```
processMarketData = filterRelevantStocks
                >>> calculateMovingAverages
```

```
>>> detectPatterns
>>> generateTradingSignals
```

Each function is pure, making the system:

- Easy to test (predictable outputs)

- Easy to parallelize (no shared state)

- Easy to debug (transparent data flow)

Strengths and Trade-offs

Major Strengths:

- Predictability: Pure functions always produce the same output for the same input

- Testability: Isolated functions are easy to test

- Concurrency: No shared state means easier parallel processing

- Composability: Functions can be combined like building blocks

Potential Challenges:

- Learning curve for developers used to imperative programming

- Performance overhead for some immutable data structures

- Memory usage in long transformation chains

- Complexity in handling stateful operations

When to Choose Logic Programming

Logic programming offers unique advantages for certain types of problems. Let's see where it really shines.

Ideal Scenarios

Logic programming excels when:

Relationship-Heavy Problems:

- Complex querying needs

- Pattern matching requirements

- Rule-based systems

- Knowledge representation

Example: Medical Diagnosis System Consider this Prolog-style rule system:

```
diagnosis(Patient, Condition) :-
            has_symptom(Patient, fever),
            has_symptom(Patient, cough),
            recent_travel(Patient, Region),
            risk_factor(Region, Condition).
```

This approach offers:

- Natural expression of medical rules

- Easy addition of new conditions

- Automatic backward chaining

- Explainable results

Strengths and Trade-offs

Major Strengths:

- Declarative rules that mirror human reasoning

- Powerful pattern matching capabilities

- Built-in search and backtracking

- Excellent for prototype development

Potential Challenges:

- Performance can be unpredictable

- Scaling challenges with large datasets

- Steeper learning curve for most developers

- Limited ecosystem compared to mainstream languages

When to Choose Answer Set Programming

ASP brings unique capabilities to certain problem classes. Let's explore its sweet spots.

Ideal Scenarios

ASP is particularly effective for:

Constraint Satisfaction Problems:

- Schedule optimization

- Resource allocation

- Configuration problems

- Planning tasks

Example: University Timetabling Consider this ASP-style scheduling problem:

```
% Each course needs one time slot
1 { schedule(Course, Time) : time_slot(Time) } 1 :-
    course(Course).

% No professor can teach two courses at once
:- schedule(C1, T), schedule(C2, T), teaches(Prof, C1)
   , teaches(Prof, C2), C1 != C2.

% Rooms must not be double-booked
:- schedule(C1, T), schedule(C2, T), assigned_room(C1,
    R), assigned_room(C2, R), C1 != C2.
```

This elegantly handles:

- Complex scheduling constraints

- Resource conflicts

- Optimization goals

- Multiple valid solutions

Strengths and Trade-offs

Major Strengths:

- Natural expression of constraints

- Finds all valid solutions

- Built-in optimization capabilities

- Separation of problem description from solving

Potential Challenges:

- NP-hard problems can be computationally intensive

- Limited to finite domains

- Requires specialized solvers

- May need careful problem modeling for efficiency

Hybrid Approaches

Sometimes the best solution is a combination of paradigms. Let's explore how to mix and match effectively.

Common Hybrid Patterns

Functional + Logic: Perfect for systems that need both data transformation and reasoning:

- Data cleanup in functional style

- Logic programming for relationship analysis

- Functional processing of logic results

Example: Smart City Traffic Management

```
-- Data types
data SensorReading = SensorReading
    { zone :: Zone
    , vehicleCount :: Int
    , timestamp :: UTCTime
    } deriving (Show, Eq)

-- Functional part: Process sensor data
processSensorData :: [SensorReading] -> [(Zone, Int)]
processSensorData = aggregateByZone
                  . filterAnomalies
                  . normalizeReadings
  where
    normalizeReadings :: [SensorReading] -> [
        SensorReading]
    normalizeReadings = filter isValidReading . map
        calibrate

    filterAnomalies :: [SensorReading] -> [
        SensorReading]
    filterAnomalies readings =
```

```
filter (\r -> vehicleCount r <=
    maxVehicleThreshold) readings

aggregateByZone :: [SensorReading] -> [(Zone, Int)
    ]
aggregateByZone = Map.toList
        . Map.fromListWith (+)
        . map (\r -> (zone r,
            vehicleCount r))
```

```
% Logic part: Traffic rule analysis
congested(Zone) :- vehicle_count(Zone, Count),
    threshold(Zone, Limit), Count > Limit.
```

ASP + Functional: Useful for optimization problems with complex data preparation:

- Functional preprocessing of input data

- ASP for constraint solving

- Functional postprocessing of solutions

Integration Strategies

How to make different paradigms work together:

Communication Patterns:

- Data interchange formats (JSON, XML)

- Inter-process communication

- Shared memory spaces

- Message queues

Architecture Considerations:

- Clear boundaries between paradigms

- Well-defined interfaces

- Error handling across boundaries

- Performance impact of transitions

Real-World Applications and Implementation Strategies

Let's dive into some concrete examples and practical guidance for implementing declarative solutions in the real world.

Case Studies

Case Study 1: E-commerce Recommendation Engine

A modern e-commerce platform combining multiple paradigms:

System Requirements:

- Real-time product recommendations

- Complex business rules

- High throughput

- Personalization

Solution Architecture:

1. Functional Programming Component:

    - User behavior data processing

    - Feature extraction

    - Score calculation

2. Logic Programming Component:

- Product relationship rules
- Category hierarchies
- Compatibility checks

Implementation Highlights: Implementation Highlights:

```
-- Data types
data UserEvent = UserEvent
    { userId :: UserId
    , productId :: ProductId
    , eventType :: EventType
    , timestamp :: UTCTime
    } deriving (Show, Eq)

-- Process user behavior
processUserEvents :: [UserEvent] -> [(ProductId,
    Double)]
processUserEvents = calculateAffinity
                  . groupByProduct
                  . filterRecentEvents

-- Individual processing steps
filterRecentEvents :: [UserEvent] -> [UserEvent]
filterRecentEvents events =
    filter isRecent events
  where
    isRecent event =
        diffUTCTime now (timestamp event) <= threshold

groupByProduct :: [UserEvent] -> Map ProductId [
    UserEvent]
```

```
groupByProduct =
    Map.groupBy productId

calculateAffinity :: Map ProductId [UserEvent] -> [(
    ProductId, Double)]
calculateAffinity =
    Map.toList . Map.map computeScore
  where
    computeScore events =
        sum $ map (weightByEventType . eventType)
            events
```

```
% Logic: Product relationships
    recommends(P1, P2) :- complementary(P1, P2),
        inStock(P2), priceRange(P2, UserBudget).
```

Results and Lessons:

- 40% improvement in recommendation relevance

- Better maintainability of business rules

- Easier A/B testing of algorithms

- Challenge: Needed careful performance tuning

Case Study 2: Hospital Resource Management

A complex healthcare scheduling system using ASP:

Challenge:

- Schedule surgeries and procedures

- Manage staff rotations

- Handle emergency cases

- Maintain equipment availability

ASP Solution:

```
% Basic scheduling rules
1 { assign(Surgery, Room, T) :
available_room(Room, T) } 1 :- pending_surgery(Surgery
    ).

% Staff constraints
:- assign(Surgery1, _, T), assign(Surgery2, _, T),
    requires_surgeon(Surgery1, Doctor),
    requires_surgeon(Surgery2, Doctor), Surgery1 !=
    Surgery2.

% Emergency handling
#maximize { 1@3, Surgery : assign(Surgery, _, _),
    emergency(Surgery) }.
```

Outcomes:

- 25% reduction in scheduling conflicts

- Better emergency response time

- Improved resource utilization

- Increased staff satisfaction

Implementation Best Practices

Development Workflow

How to approach declarative projects effectively:

Project Setup:

1. Problem Analysis

    • Map requirements to paradigms
    • Identify integration points
    • Plan data flows

2. Prototype Phase

    • Build small proof-of-concepts
    • Test paradigm boundaries
    • Measure performance

3. Implementation

    • Start with core functionality
    • Add complexity gradually
    • Maintain paradigm separation

Testing Strategies

Different paradigms require different testing approaches:

Functional Components:

- Unit tests for pure functions

- Property-based testing

- Pipeline integration tests

Logic Components:

- Rule coverage testing

- Edge case validation

- Performance benchmarking

ASP Components:

- Constraint satisfaction tests

- Solution quality metrics

- Scalability testing

Performance Optimization

Common Performance Challenges

Understanding and addressing performance bottlenecks:

Functional Programming:

- Memory pressure from immutability

- Pipeline optimization

- Garbage collection tuning

- Parallel processing overhead

Optimization Techniques:

- Lazy evaluation

- Stream fusion

- Tail recursion optimization

- Memoization

Logic Programming:

- Query optimization

- Index selection

- Cut placement

- Memory management

ASP Optimization:

- Problem decomposition

- Symmetry breaking

- Heuristic guidance

- Incremental solving

Future Trends and Considerations

Emerging Applications

Where declarative approaches are gaining traction:

AI and Machine Learning:

- Neural network architecture search

- Feature engineering pipelines

- Automated reasoning systems

- Explainable AI components

Cloud Computing:

- Infrastructure as Code

- Serverless computing

- Resource orchestration

- Policy enforcement

Integration with Modern Technologies

How declarative approaches fit with current trends:

Microservices:

- Service composition

- API design
- State management
- Event processing

DevOps:

- Configuration management
- Deployment rules
- Monitoring and alerts
- Automated recovery

Conclusion

The declarative toolbox offers powerful approaches for modern software development. Success lies in:

- Understanding your problem domain

- Choosing appropriate paradigms

- Implementing with best practices

- Continuous optimization

- Staying current with trends

Remember, the goal isn't to force a particular paradigm, but to choose the right tool for each part of your problem. Sometimes that means using one approach, sometimes it means combining several. The key is maintaining flexibility while leveraging the strengths of each paradigm.

Embracing the Declarative Future

I've got something important to tell you about where programming is heading. We've spent all this time exploring these different declarative approaches - functional programming, logic programming, ASP - and you might be wondering, "Okay, but what's the big picture here?"

The reality is, our world is getting more complex, and our old imperative ways of telling computers exactly what to do, step by step, just isn't cutting it anymore. We need to be able to think and program at a higher level. That's where declarative programming shines - it lets us focus on what we want to accomplish, not every tiny detail of how to get there.

Think about all the tools and frameworks you use today. Notice how many of them are moving toward declarative approaches? That's not a coincidence. From building web interfaces to training AI models to handling massive datasets, declarative programming is becoming the go-to approach for handling complexity.

Let's look at where this is all headed and how you can prepare for this declarative future.

Modern Applications and Frameworks

Functional Programming's Impact

Remember our exploration of Haskell's pure functions and immutability? These concepts have revolutionized modern software development in ways you might not expect. Let's look at some mind-bending examples.

Consider **React**, the popular UI framework. When Facebook's engineers were grappling with complex user interfaces, they had an epiphany that echoed functional programming principles: what if a UI was just a pure function of state? Look at this transformation:

```javascript
// Traditional imperative async code
async function handleUserData() {
    try {
        const response = await fetch('/api/user');
        const userData = await response.json();
        updateUI(userData);
    } catch (error) {
        handleError(error);
    }
}

// Functional chain of transformations
fetch('/api/user')
    .then(response => response.json())
    .then(user => updateUI(user))
    .catch(error => handleError(error));
```

This chain of operations demonstrates how functional programming's core concept of function composition, which we explored in our Haskell chapter, has influenced modern JavaScript. Just as we saw how functions can be chained together to transform data in Haskell, modern JavaScript frameworks adopt this same pattern of clean data transformation.

Even state management libraries like **Redux** took inspiration from functional programming:

```
// Redux reducer - pure function, just like in Haskell
const reducer = (state, action) => {
    switch (action.type) {
        case 'INCREMENT':
            return { ...state, count: state.count + 1
                };
        case 'DECREMENT':
            return { ...state, count: state.count - 1
                };
        default:
            return state;
    }
};
```

This pattern of immutable state transformations through pure functions is directly inspired by functional programming principles. I remember reading an article about Redux, where its creator Dan Abramov was asked about his influences, and he explicitly cited functional programming concepts.

In cloud computing, functional thinking has led to the serverless revolution. **AWS** Lambda and similar services treat entire applications as pure functions that transform inputs to outputs:

```
exports.handler = async (event) => {
    const result = await processData(event.data);
    return {
        statusCode: 200,
        body: JSON.stringify(result)
    };
};
```

This is functional programming at a system level – each function is stateless, side-effects are minimized, and composition is key. The same principles we learned with Haskell are now organizing entire cloud architectures.

Logic Programming's Renaissance

Remember how Prolog allowed us to express relationships and let the system figure out solutions? This declarative approach to knowledge representation and querying is experiencing a fascinating revival in modern systems.

Take **GraphQL**, for instance. While it might look like just another query language, its core idea mirrors Prolog's declarative querying:

Prolog-style relationship definition:

```
parent(john, mary).
parent(mary, ann).
ancestor(X, Y) :- parent(X, Y).
ancestor(X, Y) :- parent(X, Z), ancestor(Z, Y).
```

GraphQL:

```
// GraphQL Schema
type Person {
  id: ID!
  name: String!
  children: [Person]
  descendants: [Person]
}

// GraphQL data
{
  "persons": [
    {
      "name": "john",
      "children": [
        { "name": "mary" }
      ]
    },
    {
      "name": "mary",
      "children": [
        { "name": "ann" }
      ]
    },
    {
      "name": "ann",
      "children": []
    }
  ]
}

type Query {
  person(name: String!): Person
```

```
    ancestors(personName: String!): [Person]
}

// GraphQL query
query {
    user(id: "john") {
        children {
            children {
                name
            }
        }
    }
}
```

In both cases, we're declaring what relationships we want to traverse, not how to traverse them. The system figures out the optimal query plan, just as Prolog's resolution engine determines the search strategy.

Natural Language Processing systems are increasingly using logic programming concepts. Consider how modern chatbots handle intent recognition:

Prolog-style rules for mortgage qualification:

```
can_help(Customer, mortgage) :-
    has_income(Customer, Income),
    Income > 50000,
    credit_score(Customer, Score),
    Score > 700.
```

Modern intent matching system (e.g., in a chatbot)

```
intents:
```

```
- mortgage_inquiry:
    conditions:
      - income > 50000
      - credit_score > 700
    response: "You may qualify for our mortgage
      products"
```

The declarative nature of logic programming makes it perfect for building knowledge graphs, which are becoming crucial in AI systems:

Prolog-style knowledge representation:

```
works_at(john, microsoft).
expertise(john, python).
requires(project_x, python).
suitable_for(Person, Project) :- requires(Project,
    Skill), expertise(Person, Skill).
```

Modern knowledge graph query (**SPARQL**):

```
SELECT ?person
WHERE {
    ?person works_at "Microsoft" .
    ?person has_skill "Python" .
    ?project requires "Python" .
}
```

Answer Set Programming's Emerging Applications

The power of ASP in handling complex constraints and optimization problems is finding new applications in modern system design. Remember how we used ASP to solve puzzle-like problems? Now, similar techniques are being used to solve real-world scheduling and resource allocation problems in cloud systems:

ASP-style container scheduling:

```
container(c1). container(c2). container(c3).
node(n1). node(n2).
memory(n1,8). memory(n2,16).
requires(c1,4). requires(c2,6). requires(c3,8).

1 { assign(C,N) : node(N) } 1 :- container(C).
:- node(N), Sum = #sum { M,C : assign(C,N), requires(C
    ,M) }, memory(N,MaxMem), Sum > MaxMem.
```

Modern **Kubernetes** scheduling constraints:

```
apiVersion: v1
kind: Pod
metadata:
  name: memory-demo
spec:
  containers:
    - name: memory-demo-ctr
      resources:
        limits:
          memory: "200Mi"
        requests:
          memory: "100Mi"
```

ASP's approach to constraint solving is revolutionizing infrastructure configuration management. Instead of writing imperative scripts, we can declare constraints and let the system find valid configurations:

ASP network configuration:

```
node(web1;web2;db1).
connection(X,Y) :- node(X), node(Y), X != Y.
:- connection(X,Y), not secure_channel(X,Y).
:- node(X), count { Y : connection(X,Y) } > 3.
```

Modern infrastructure as code (**Terraform**):

```
resource "aws_security_group" "example" {
    name = "example"
    ingress {
        from_port = 443
        to_port = 443
        protocol = "tcp"
        cidr_blocks = ["0.0.0.0/0"]
    }
}
```

In autonomous systems and robotics, ASP's ability to handle complex rules and constraints is proving invaluable. Consider this example of robot navigation planning:

ASP path planning:

```
position(robot,X,Y,T+1) :- move(D,T), position(robot,
    X1,Y1,T), nextpos(D,X1,Y1,X,Y), not obstacle(X,Y).
:- position(robot,X,Y,T), obstacle(X,Y).
```

Modern autonomous navigation system:

```
navigation_constraints:
    avoid_obstacles: true
    maintain_safe_distance: 2.0
    prefer_known_paths: true
```

```
optimize:
    minimize_travel_time: true
    minimize_energy_consumption: true
```

The Role of Declarative Programming in AI

Let me share something fascinating about how these declarative approaches we've been studying are becoming crucial in AI. Each one brings something special to the table - let me show you what I mean.

Functional Programming in Machine Learning

You know how functional programming helped us write cleaner, more predictable code? Well, guess what - it's doing the same thing for machine learning pipelines. Look at these two approaches:

Here's the old way:

```python
def process_data(data):
    cleaned = []
    for item in data:
        if not item.is_null():
            normalized = normalize(item)
            cleaned.append(normalized)
    return cleaned
```

And here's the functional way:

```python
def process_data(data):
    return (data.filter(lambda x: not x.is_null())
                .map(normalize)
                .collect())
```

Pretty different, right? And check out how modern ML frameworks like TensorFlow and PyTorch are using these ideas:

```
# Look how clean this is!
model = nn.Sequential(
    nn.Linear(input_size, 128),
    nn.ReLU(),
    nn.Linear(128, output_size)
)
```

Logic Programming in AI Reasoning

Remember all that pattern matching we did in Prolog? It's making a comeback in modern AI systems. Here's what I mean:

Old-school Prolog:

```
symptom(flu, fever).
symptom(flu, cough).
symptom(covid, fever).
symptom(covid, cough).
symptom(covid, loss_of_taste).

has_condition(Patient, Condition) :-
    findall(S, symptom(Condition, S), Symptoms),
    patient_has_all_symptoms(Patient, Symptoms).
```

Modern AI diagnostic systems are using similar ideas, just in a more accessible format:

```
rules:
    if:
        symptoms:
```

```
            - fever
            - cough
            - loss_of_taste
        then:
            suggest_diagnosis: "COVID-19"
            confidence: 0.85
```

See how these old ideas are finding new life? It's not just about knowing the syntax - it's about understanding these powerful ways of thinking about problems.

ASP in Explainable AI

Here's something really interesting about ASP - it's becoming a game-changer in making AI systems that can actually explain themselves. Instead of trying to figure out why a neural network made a decision (good luck with that!), we can write clear rules that show our reasoning:

```
% Here's how we might make and explain loan decisions
approve_loan(Customer) :-
    income(Customer, I),
    I > 50000,
    credit_score(Customer, S),
    S > 700,
    not has_defaults(Customer).

% And here's the cool part - built-in explanations
explain(Customer, approved) :-
    approve_loan(Customer),
    income(Customer, I),
    credit_score(Customer, S),
```

```
    format("Approved: Income=$~w, Score=~w", [I, S]).

explain(Customer, rejected) :-
    not approve_loan(Customer),
    income(Customer, I),
    credit_score(Customer, S),
    format("Rejected: Required income>50000, score>700
        ").
```

See what we did there? When someone asks "Why did the AI make this decision?", we can give them a straight answer. This is huge in fields like finance, healthcare, and anywhere else where you need to justify automated decisions. It's one of the reasons I'm so excited about combining ASP with modern AI systems - we get the power of AI with the clarity of logical rules. In fact, my PhD work focused on developing ASP-based commonsense reasoning systems and building ASP solvers, so I've seen firsthand how powerful these techniques can be.

Career Opportunities in the Age of AI

You know, one of the main reasons I decided to write this book was something that's been keeping me up at nights lately. Have you noticed how tools like ChatGPT and Claude are getting better and better at writing code? It's pretty mind-blowing - and honestly, a bit scary if you're a traditional programmer like I used to be.

Let me be direct here: I think we're at a turning point in our industry. Those jobs where we spend all day writing basic CRUD applications or implementing standard algorithms? A lot of that work is going to be automated away. I'm not saying this to frighten you - I'm saying it because I want you to be prepared.

But here's the exciting part: while some doors are closing, others are opening wide. That's exactly why I've spent so much time showing you these declarative paradigms. The future isn't about competing with AI to write code - it's about working alongside AI, speaking its language, and operating at a higher level of abstraction.

Think about it - when you're working with these AI tools, you're not writing out every line of code anymore. You're describing what you want to achieve, specifying constraints, and thinking about systems at a higher level. Sound familiar? That's exactly what we've been practicing with functional, logic, and answer set programming!

Let me show you how the skills (at least the "views") we've built up through this book map directly to the opportunities I see emerging...

Transferable Skills

Remember all those mental models we've been developing through our journey? They're not just academic exercises - they're your toolkit for the AI age:

First, think about what we learned from functional programming. It's not just about those fancy map and reduce functions, right? It's about seeing software as a series of transformations, understanding why immutability matters, and how we can build complex systems by combining simple parts. I can't tell you how many times this way of thinking has helped me architect data pipelines that actually make sense!

Then there's what we picked up from logic programming. Remember when we first looked at Prolog and you might have thought "When am I ever going to use this?" Well, turns out those skills – modeling relationships, thinking declaratively, understanding pattern matching – they're gold when you're working with modern knowledge systems and AI.

And don't get me started on what ASP taught us! That whole approach to thinking in constraints and optimization? It's exactly what you need when you're dealing with complex system requirements or resource allocation problems.

Emerging Roles

Let me tell you about some of the exciting roles I'm seeing pop up in the industry. These aren't just job titles - they're opportunities to apply everything we've been learning:

Take AI/ML Engineers, for instance. Sure, everyone's talking about machine learning, but here's what they don't tell you: success in this field isn't just about understanding neural networks. It's about building robust data pipelines (hello, functional programming!), representing knowledge effectively (thanks, logic programming!), and handling complex constraints (ASP to the rescue!).

Or look at Cloud Architects. Gone are the days of manually configuring servers. Now it's all declarative – you specify what you want, and the system figures out how to make it happen. Sound familiar? It's exactly the mindset we've been cultivating throughout this book.

And Data Engineers – they're not just SQL jockeys anymore. They need to think in terms of transformations (functional programming), understand how to model complex relationships (logic programming), and optimize data flows (ASP principles).

Future Trends

Let me share something interesting I've been noticing in the industry lately:

Have you seen these Low-Code/No-Code platforms? They're

everywhere now! But here's the thing – they're not dumbing down programming; they're making it more declarative. If you understand the principles we've covered, you'll see these platforms for what they really are: declarative interfaces to complex systems.

And AI-assisted programming – this is where everything we've learned comes together. When you're working with AI tools, you need to be crystal clear about your intentions. It's not about writing every line of code anymore; it's about effectively communicating what you want to achieve. Sounds a lot like declarative programming, doesn't it?

The most exciting trend I'm seeing is in Complex Systems Design. As systems get more complicated, the old imperative way of specifying every detail just doesn't cut it anymore. We need to think at a higher level, focus on what we want to achieve rather than how to achieve it. This is exactly what we've been practicing!

You know what really excites me about all this? The future of programming isn't about writing more code – it's about expressing intent more clearly. All those hours we spent wrestling with functional programming concepts, figuring out logic programming puzzles, and understanding ASP – they weren't just exercises. They were preparation for this new era of software development.

I truly believe that the skills we've developed through this journey aren't just going to help you survive in the age of AI – they're going to help you thrive. Because while AI might be great at writing individual lines of code, it still needs humans who can think clearly about problems, express solutions declaratively, and understand the bigger picture.

Conclusion: The Convergence of Declarative Paradigms

You know what's fascinating? As we're wrapping up our journey through these three paradigms, I'm seeing something really exciting happening in the industry. These approaches – functional, logic, and answer set programming – aren't just living in their own separate worlds anymore. They're coming together in ways that I think are going to change how we build software.

The Synthesis of Approaches

Let me show you what I mean. Take a look at this example of a modern AI system:

```
# Here's the functional part - looks familiar, right?
def preprocess_data(data):
    return (data
            .map(normalize)
            .filter(validate)
            .collect())

# And now some logic-based rules - remember our Prolog
    adventures?
rules = {
    "credit_worthy": """
        eligible(Customer) :-
            income(Customer, I), I > 50000,
            credit_score(Customer, S), S > 700.
    """
```

```
}

# And here's where ASP comes in - just like we learned
    !
constraints = """
    % Resource allocation constraints
    {assign(Task, Resource)} = 1 :- task(Task).
    :- resource(R),
        total_load(R, L), capacity(R, C), L > C.
"""
```

See what's happening here? These paradigms are playing together beautifully! It's like they're borrowing the best ideas from each other. Remember how we talked about immutability in functional programming? That same concept helps make ASP's stable models work better. And all that pattern matching we did in logic programming? It's making functional programming even more powerful.

The Road Ahead

Want to see something really cool? Here's what I think the future might look like:

```
# Check this out - declarative AI specifications
system = AI.specify("""
    Goals:
        - Maximize customer satisfaction
        - Minimize resource usage
    Constraints:
        - Never exceed budget of $10000
        - Maintain 99.9% uptime
```

```
    Learning:
        - From customer feedback
        - From system metrics
""")

# And imagine programming environments that let us mix
    and match:
@functional
def process_data(stream):
    return stream.transform(...)

@logic
def derive_insights(data):
    """
    insight(X) :- pattern(X, P), threshold(P, T).
    """

@constraints
def allocate_resources(demands):
    """
    {assign(D, R)} = 1 :- demand(D).
    """
```

Pretty neat, right? We're moving toward a world where we can use the best tool for each part of our problem, all within the same system.

Final Thoughts

You know, as I'm writing this final section, I keep thinking about how far we've come. Remember when we first started talking about functional programming, and maybe some of those concepts seemed a bit abstract? Or when we dove into logic programming and you might have wondered, "Where am I ever going to use this?"

But look at what you've gained:

- From functional programming, you learned to see everything as data transformations

- Logic programming taught you how to express complex relationships clearly

- And ASP? It showed you how to think in terms of constraints and solutions

Here's what I really want you to take away from all this: We're not just learning different programming styles – we're learning different ways of thinking about problems. And in a world where AI can increasingly handle the "how," our ability to clearly express the "what" becomes incredibly valuable.

Keep Exploring!

Before we wrap up, here are some things I'd encourage you to try:

1. Next time you're working on a project, try mixing these approaches. Maybe use functional programming for your data pipeline, but throw in some logic programming for your business rules.

2. Keep an eye on new declarative frameworks – they're popping up everywhere!

3. Play around with AI tools, but apply what you've learned about declarative thinking.

4. Practice expressing problems declaratively – it's a skill that gets better with use.

You know what? The end of this book isn't really an ending at all. It's more like you've just gotten a new set of powerful tools, and now the fun part begins – using them to build amazing things.

I'd love to hear about how you end up using these ideas in your own work. Remember, the future is declarative, and you're now well-equipped to be part of shaping it!

Epilogue

As we close this journey through declarative programming, let's reflect on a profound realization: the declarative approach may well be the natural language of true artificial intelligence.

Consider what we mean by "intelligence." When we program computers to follow step-by-step instructions blindly, are we really creating intelligence? Or are we merely constructing sophisticated automatons – artificial idiots that execute commands without understanding? True intelligence isn't about following instructions; it's about understanding goals and independently finding paths to achieve them.

The emergence of Large Language Models like ChatGPT, Claude, and Gemini offers us a glimpse into this future. Think about how we interact with these systems – we tell them what we have and what we want, and they figure out the path forward. Isn't this fundamentally declarative? We're not instructing them on how to solve problems; we're declaring our desired outcomes.

Yet, we're still in the awkward teenage years of this technology. "Prompt engineering" has emerged as a crucial skill, but let's be honest – it's more art than science. It lacks the rigor and reproducibility that we've come to expect from engineering disciplines. In the classical AI community, we have a more scientific approach called "knowledge engineering," which offers formal methods for representing and manipulating knowledge.

What I envision for the future is the emergence of a formalized declarative language for AI interaction. This isn't just about making prompts more reliable – it's about creating a structured way to express problems and desired outcomes. This language would allow us to specify not just what we want, but also the constraints, validation criteria, and boundaries within which solutions must operate.

The future of AI isn't about teaching machines to follow our instructions better – it's about enabling them to understand our goals and independently devise solutions. The declarative approach isn't just a programming paradigm; it's the natural language of true artificial intelligence.

As we stand at this technological crossroads, remember this: computers that blindly follow step-by-step instructions aren't intelligent – they're just complex calculators. True AI will emerge when we can simply declare our goals and trust the system to find the best path forward. The declarative approach we've explored in this book isn't just a way of programming – it's a glimpse into the future of human-AI interaction.

Perhaps the most profound insight is this: declarative thinking isn't just another tool in our programming toolkit. It's the key to unlocking true artificial intelligence, where machines don't just follow our instructions, but truly understand our intent and autonomously work toward our goals.

The future is declarative. And it's already beginning.

Fang Li
Thanksgiving Day, 2024
Edmond, Oklahoma

Disclaimer

This book was written with the assistance of artificial intelligence tools for grammar correction and example code implementation. While every effort has been made to ensure originality, if any content or code examples bear similarity to existing works, this is purely coincidental and unintentional.

The code examples in this book are provided for educational purposes only. Neither the author nor the publisher makes any warranties about the functionality or safety of the code, and they cannot be held liable for any damages or consequences from using the information contained in this book.

All views expressed are my own and do not represent the opinions of any entity whatsoever with which I have been, am now, or will be affiliated. The content is provided "as is" without warranty of any kind, either express or implied.

Appendix: Fun Implementation Examples

Throughout this book, we have explored the theoretical foundations and principles of declarative programming. Now, in this final appendix, we bring theory into practice by presenting fifteen concrete implementations across three major declarative paradigms: Functional Programming (Haskell), Logic Programming (Prolog), and Answer Set Programming (Clingo). For each paradigm, we showcase five carefully selected examples that demonstrate how declarative approaches elegantly solve real-world problems. Each example includes a problem description followed by its implementation, allowing readers to see how the concepts discussed in previous chapters materialize into working solutions.

All example codes are available at: `https://github.com/fanglioc/the_declarative_mind`

Functional Programming with Haskell

Example 1: N-Queens Problem

Problem Description

Place N queens on an N×N chessboard so that no two queens threaten each other. This means no two queens can share the same row, column, or diagonal. The problem demonstrates list comprehension and recursive problem solving in functional programming.

Implementation

```haskell
-- N-Queens Solver in Haskell
-- A queen's position is represented by (row, column)
type Position = (Int, Int)

-- Check if a queen can attack another queen
threatens :: Position -> Position -> Bool
threatens (r1, c1) (r2, c2) =
    r1 == r2 ||                    -- Same row
    c1 == c2 ||                    -- Same column
    abs (r1 - r2) == abs (c1 - c2)  -- Same diagonal

-- Check if a queen position is safe with respect to
   existing queens
isSafe :: Position -> [Position] -> Bool
isSafe pos = not . any (threatens pos)
```

```haskell
-- Generate all solutions for n queens
queens :: Int -> [[Position]]
queens n = queensHelper n n
    where
        queensHelper :: Int -> Int -> [[Position]]
        queensHelper n row
            | row == 0 = [[]]   -- Base case: empty
                solution
            | otherwise = [      -- For each row
                (row, col) : others |
                others <- queensHelper n (row-1),
                    -- Recursive solutions
                col <- [1..n],
                    -- Try each column
                isSafe (row, col) others
                    -- Check if safe
            ]

-- Pretty print a solution
printBoard :: [Position] -> IO ()
printBoard qs = mapM_ printRow [1..n]
    where
        n = length qs
        printRow row = do
            putStrLn [if (row, col) `elem` qs then 'Q'
                else '.' | col <- [1..n]]

-- Main function to print first solution
main :: IO ()
main = do
    let n = 8   -- Try 8-queens puzzle
    case queens n of
        (solution:_) -> do
```

```
      putStrLn $ "A solution for " ++ show n ++
         "-queens:"
      printBoard solution
[] -> putStrLn "No solution exists"
```

Example 2: Binary Search Tree Operations

Problem Description

Implement a binary search tree with basic operations like insertion, deletion, searching, and traversal. This demonstrates how functional programming handles data structures and recursive operations.

Implementation

```haskell
-- Binary Search Tree implementation in Haskell
data Tree a = Empty | Node a (Tree a) (Tree a)
    deriving (Show, Eq)

-- Insert a value into the BST
insert :: Ord a => a -> Tree a -> Tree a
insert x Empty = Node x Empty Empty
insert x (Node value left right)
    | x < value  = Node value (insert x left) right
    | x > value  = Node value left (insert x right)
    | otherwise  = Node value left right  -- No
        duplicates


-- Search for a value in the BST
search :: Ord a => a -> Tree a -> Bool
search _ Empty = False
search x (Node value left right)
    | x == value = True
    | x < value  = search x left
    | otherwise  = search x right
```

```
-- Tree traversals
inorder :: Tree a -> [a]
inorder Empty = []
inorder (Node value left right) = inorder left ++ [
    value] ++ inorder right

preorder :: Tree a -> [a]
preorder Empty = []
preorder (Node value left right) = [value] ++ preorder
    left ++ preorder right

postorder :: Tree a -> [a]
postorder Empty = []
postorder (Node value left right) = postorder left ++
    postorder right ++ [value]

-- Find minimum value in a non-empty tree
findMin :: Tree a -> a
findMin (Node value Empty _) = value
findMin (Node _ left _) = findMin left

-- Delete a value from the BST
delete :: Ord a => a -> Tree a -> Tree a
delete _ Empty = Empty
delete x (Node value left right)
    | x < value   = Node value (delete x left) right
    | x > value   = Node value left (delete x right)
    | otherwise   = case (left, right) of
        (Empty, Empty) -> Empty
        (Empty, _)      -> right
        (_, Empty)      -> left
        _               -> Node minRight left (delete
            minRight right)
```

```
                              where minRight = findMin right

-- Example usage
main :: IO ()
main = do
    let tree = foldr insert Empty [5,3,7,1,9,2,8]
    putStrLn $ "Inorder traversal: " ++ show (inorder
        tree)
    putStrLn $ "Search for 3: " ++ show (search 3 tree
        )
    putStrLn $ "Search for 4: " ++ show (search 4 tree
        )
    let newTree = delete 3 tree
    putStrLn $ "After deleting 3: " ++ show (inorder
        newTree)
```

Example 3: Advanced List Operations

Problem Description

Implement a collection of custom list operations that demonstrate the power of functional programming concepts like map, filter, fold, and list comprehension. This shows how to process data functionally without mutable state.

Implementation

```haskell
-- Advanced List Operations in Haskell

-- Custom implementation of map using recursion
myMap :: (a -> b) -> [a] -> [b]
myMap _ [] = []
myMap f (x:xs) = f x : myMap f xs

-- Custom implementation of filter
myFilter :: (a -> Bool) -> [a] -> [a]
myFilter _ [] = []
myFilter p (x:xs)
    | p x       = x : myFilter p xs
    | otherwise = myFilter p xs

-- Custom implementation of foldl
myFoldl :: (b -> a -> b) -> b -> [a] -> b
myFoldl _ acc [] = acc
myFoldl f acc (x:xs) = myFoldl f (f acc x) xs

-- Custom implementation of foldr
myFoldr :: (a -> b -> b) -> b -> [a] -> b
```

```
myFoldr _ acc [] = acc
myFoldr f acc (x:xs) = f x (myFoldr f acc xs)

-- Advanced list operations

-- Zip with function (zipWith)
myZipWith :: (a -> b -> c) -> [a] -> [b] -> [c]
myZipWith _ [] _ = []
myZipWith _ _ [] = []
myZipWith f (x:xs) (y:ys) = f x y : myZipWith f xs ys

-- Group consecutive elements
group :: Eq a => [a] -> [[a]]
group [] = []
group (x:xs) = let (same, different) = span (== x) xs
               in (x:same) : group different

-- Custom take while with predicate
myTakeWhile :: (a -> Bool) -> [a] -> [a]
myTakeWhile _ [] = []
myTakeWhile p (x:xs)
    | p x       = x : myTakeWhile p xs
    | otherwise = []

-- Generate all subsequences of a list
subsequences :: [a] -> [[a]]
subsequences [] = [[]]
subsequences (x:xs) = let sub = subsequences xs
                      in sub ++ map (x:) sub

-- Example usage and testing
main :: IO ()
main = do
```

```
-- Test myMap
putStrLn "Testing myMap:"
print $ myMap (*2) [1..5]

-- Test myFilter
putStrLn "\nTesting myFilter:"
print $ myFilter even [1..10]

-- Test folds
putStrLn "\nTesting folds:"
print $ myFoldl (+) 0 [1..5]
print $ myFoldr (:) [] [1..5]

-- Test zipWith
putStrLn "\nTesting myZipWith:"
print $ myZipWith (+) [1,2,3] [4,5,6]

-- Test group
putStrLn "\nTesting group:"
print $ group [1,1,1,2,2,3,3,3,3]

-- Test takeWhile
putStrLn "\nTesting myTakeWhile:"
print $ myTakeWhile (<5) [1..10]

-- Test subsequences
putStrLn "\nTesting subsequences:"
print $ subsequences [1,2,3]
```

Example 4: Expression Evaluator

Problem Description

Implement an evaluator for mathematical expressions that can handle basic arithmetic operations, variables, and function calls. This demonstrates pattern matching and recursive evaluation in functional programming.

Implementation

```haskell
-- Mathematical Expression Evaluator

-- Define the expression data type
data Expr = Num Double
          | Add Expr Expr
          | Sub Expr Expr
          | Mul Expr Expr
          | Div Expr Expr
          | Pow Expr Expr
          | Var String
          | Fun String Expr    -- Function application (e
                .g., sin, cos)
          deriving Show

-- Environment to store variable values
type Env = [(String, Double)]

-- Built-in functions
type FunDef = Double -> Double

-- Map of available functions
```

```
functions :: [(String, FunDef)]
functions = [
    ("sin", sin),
    ("cos", cos),
    ("exp", exp),
    ("log", log),
    ("sqrt", sqrt)
    ]

-- Evaluate an expression in given environment
eval :: Env -> Expr -> Either String Double
eval _ (Num n) = Right n

eval env (Add e1 e2) = do
    v1 <- eval env e1
    v2 <- eval env e2
    Right (v1 + v2)

eval env (Sub e1 e2) = do
    v1 <- eval env e1
    v2 <- eval env e2
    Right (v1 - v2)

eval env (Mul e1 e2) = do
    v1 <- eval env e1
    v2 <- eval env e2
    Right (v1 * v2)

eval env (Div e1 e2) = do
    v1 <- eval env e1
    v2 <- eval env e2
    if v2 == 0
        then Left "Division by zero"
```

```
            else Right (v1 / v2)

eval env (Pow e1 e2) = do
    v1 <- eval env e1
    v2 <- eval env e2
    Right (v1 ** v2)

eval env (Var name) =
    case lookup name env of
        Just v  -> Right v
        Nothing -> Left $ "Undefined variable: " ++
            name

eval env (Fun name e) = do
    v <- eval env e
    case lookup name functions of
        Just f  -> Right (f v)
        Nothing -> Left $ "Undefined function: " ++
            name

-- Parse a simple expression (for demonstration)
parse :: String -> Either String Expr
parse "x" = Right (Var "x")
parse "y" = Right (Var "y")
parse s = case reads s of
    [(n, "")] -> Right (Num n)
    _         -> Left $ "Cannot parse: " ++ s

-- Example usage
main :: IO ()
main = do
    let env = [("x", 2), ("y", 3)]
    let expr1 = Add (Mul (Var "x") (Var "y")) (Num 1)
```

```
let expr2 = Fun "sin" (Div (Var "x") (Num 2))

putStrLn "Expression 1: x * y + 1"
print $ eval env expr1

putStrLn "\nExpression 2: sin(x/2)"
print $ eval env expr2

-- Test error handling
let expr3 = Div (Num 1) (Num 0)
putStrLn "\nExpression 3: 1/0"
print $ eval env expr3
```

Example 5: Infinite Sequence Generation

Problem Description

Demonstrate Haskell's lazy evaluation by implementing various infinite sequences including Fibonacci numbers, prime numbers, and other mathematical sequences. This shows how functional programming can handle potentially infinite data structures efficiently.

Implementation

```haskell
-- Infinite Sequence Generators

-- Fibonacci sequence using lazy evaluation
fibs :: [Integer]
fibs = 0 : 1 : zipWith (+) fibs (tail fibs)

-- Prime numbers using the sieve of Eratosthenes
primes :: [Integer]
primes = sieve [2..]
    where
        sieve (p:xs) = p : sieve [x | x <- xs, x `mod`
            p /= 0]

-- Collatz sequence for a given starting number
collatz :: Integer -> [Integer]
collatz 1 = [1]
collatz n = n : collatz (next n)
    where
        next x | even x     = x `div` 2
```

```
                    | otherwise  = 3 * x + 1

-- Perfect squares with their square roots
squares :: [(Integer, Integer)]
squares = [(n^2, n) | n <- [1..]]

-- Pascal's Triangle as infinite list of rows
pascal :: [[Integer]]
pascal = [1] : map nextRow pascal
    where
        nextRow row = zipWith (+) ([0] ++ row) (row ++
            [0])

-- Utility functions to work with infinite sequences
take' :: Int -> [a] -> [a]
take' n xs = take n xs

takeWhile' :: (a -> Bool) -> [a] -> [a]
takeWhile' = takeWhile

-- Find first occurrence satisfying a predicate
findFirst :: (a -> Bool) -> [a] -> Maybe a
findFirst p xs = case dropWhile (not . p) xs of
    []      -> Nothing
    (x:_) -> Just x

-- Main function demonstrating usage
main :: IO ()
main = do
    putStrLn "First 10 Fibonacci numbers:"
    print $ take 10 fibs

    putStrLn "\nFirst 10 prime numbers:"
```

```
    print $ take 10 primes

    putStrLn "\nCollatz sequence starting from 13:"
    print $ collatz 13

    putStrLn "\nFirst 5 perfect squares with their
        roots:"
    print $ take 5 squares

    putStrLn "\nFirst 5 rows of Pascal's Triangle:"
    mapM_ print $ take 5 pascal

    putStrLn "\nFirst prime number above 100:"
    print $ findFirst (>100) primes

    putStrLn "\nFibonacci numbers less than 100:"
    print $ takeWhile (<100) fibs

    putStrLn "\nFirst Fibonacci number above 1000:"
    print $ findFirst (>1000) fibs
```

Logic Programming with Prolog

Example 1: Family Relationships

Problem Description

Implement a family tree database with rules to determine various relationships (parent, grandparent, ancestor, sibling, cousin, etc.). This demonstrates Prolog's strength in expressing relationships and recursive rules.

Implementation

```
/* Family Relationships in Prolog */

/* Facts: parent(Parent, Child) */
parent(john, mary).
parent(john, ann).
parent(jane, mary).
parent(jane, ann).
parent(mary, peter).
parent(mary, paul).
parent(steve, peter).
parent(steve, paul).
parent(ann, james).
parent(ann, susan).
parent(bob, james).
parent(bob, susan).

/* Rules for different family relationships */
```

```prolog
% Father relationship
father(Father, Child) :-
    parent(Father, Child),
    male(Father).

% Mother relationship
mother(Mother, Child) :-
    parent(Mother, Child),
    female(Mother).

% Gender facts
male(john).
male(steve).
male(bob).
male(peter).
male(paul).
male(james).

female(jane).
female(mary).
female(ann).
female(susan).

% Sibling relationship
sibling(X, Y) :-
    parent(P, X),
    parent(P, Y),
    X \= Y.

% Brother relationship
brother(X, Y) :-
    sibling(X, Y),
```

```
    male(X).

% Sister relationship
sister(X, Y) :-
    sibling(X, Y),
    female(X).

% Grandparent relationship
grandparent(GP, GC) :-
    parent(GP, P),
    parent(P, GC).

% Ancestor relationship
ancestor(A, D) :-
    parent(A, D).
ancestor(A, D) :-
    parent(A, X),
    ancestor(X, D).

% Uncle/Aunt relationship
uncle_aunt(UA, NC) :-
    parent(P, NC),
    sibling(UA, P).

% Cousin relationship
cousin(X, Y) :-
    parent(P1, X),
    parent(P2, Y),
    sibling(P1, P2).

/* Example queries:
?- sibling(mary, ann).
?- grandparent(john, peter).
```

```prolog
?- ancestor(jane, james).
?- cousin(peter, james).
?- uncle_aunt(ann, peter).
*/

/* Helper predicates for testing relationships */
test_relationships(Person) :-
    write('Parents of '), write(Person), write(':'),
        nl,
    parent(Parent, Person),
    write(Parent), nl,
    fail.
test_relationships(_).

test_siblings(Person) :-
    write('Siblings of '), write(Person), write(':'),
        nl,
    sibling(Sibling, Person),
    write(Sibling), nl,
    fail.
test_siblings(_).

test_grandparents(Person) :-
    write('Grandparents of '), write(Person), write(':
        '), nl,
    grandparent(GP, Person),
    write(GP), nl,
    fail.
test_grandparents(_).
```

Example 2: Path Finding in a Graph

Problem Description

Implement a graph representation and various path-finding algorithms including shortest path, all possible paths, and paths with specific constraints. This shows Prolog's power in searching and backtracking.

Implementation

```
/* Graph Path Finding in Prolog */

/* Define the graph using edge/3 facts
   edge(From, To, Distance) */
edge(a, b, 4).
edge(a, c, 2).
edge(b, d, 3).
edge(c, d, 1).
edge(c, e, 5).
edge(d, e, 2).
edge(d, f, 6).
edge(e, f, 4).

/* Bidirectional edges */
connected(X, Y, D) :- edge(X, Y, D).
connected(X, Y, D) :- edge(Y, X, D).

/* Find a path between two nodes */
path(Start, End, Path, Distance) :-
    path(Start, End, [Start], Path, Distance).
```

```
path(End, End, Visited, Path, 0) :-
    reverse(Visited, Path).

path(Start, End, Visited, Path, Distance) :-
    connected(Start, Next, D),
    \+ member(Next, Visited),
    path(Next, End, [Next|Visited], Path, D1),
    Distance is D + D1.

/* Find shortest path using path length */
shortest_path(Start, End, Path, Distance) :-
    findall([P,D], path(Start, End, P, D), Paths),
    min_path(Paths, Path, Distance).

min_path([[Path,Dist]], Path, Dist).
min_path([[P1,D1],[_,D2]|Rest], MinPath, MinDist) :-
    D1 =< D2,
    min_path([[P1,D1]|Rest], MinPath, MinDist).
min_path([[_,D1],[P2,D2]|Rest], MinPath, MinDist) :-
    D1 > D2,
    min_path([[P2,D2]|Rest], MinPath, MinDist).

/* Find all paths with distance less than Max */
paths_under(Start, End, MaxDist, Path, Dist) :-
    path(Start, End, Path, Dist),
    Dist =< MaxDist.

/* Find paths visiting specific nodes */
path_through(Start, End, Through, Path, Distance) :-
    path(Start, Through, Path1, D1),
    path(Through, End, Path2, D2),
    append(P1, [_|P2], Path),
    append(Path1, Path2, Path),
```

```prolog
    Distance is D1 + D2.

/* Helper predicates to print paths */
print_path([]).
print_path([H|T]) :-
    write(H), write(' -> '),
    print_path(T).

/* Example usage queries:
?- path(a, f, Path, Distance).
?- shortest_path(a, f, Path, Distance).
?- paths_under(a, f, 10, Path, Distance).
?- path_through(a, f, d, Path, Distance).
*/

/* Test predicates */
test_all_paths(Start, End) :-
    write('All paths from '), write(Start),
    write(' to '), write(End), write(':'), nl,
    path(Start, End, Path, Distance),
    write('Path: '), print_path(Path), nl,
    write('Distance: '), write(Distance), nl,
    fail.
test_all_paths(_, _).

test_shortest_path(Start, End) :-
    shortest_path(Start, End, Path, Distance),
    write('Shortest path from '), write(Start),
    write(' to '), write(End), write(':'), nl,
    write('Path: '), print_path(Path), nl,
    write('Distance: '), write(Distance), nl.
```

Example 3: Expert System

Problem Description

Implement a simple expert system for diagnosing computer problems. This demonstrates Prolog's natural ability to model expert knowledge and inference rules.

Implementation

```prolog
/* Computer Problem Diagnosis Expert System */

/* Facts about symptoms and their related problems */
symptom(wont_boot, 'Computer won\'t start').
symptom(blue_screen, 'Blue screen error').
symptom(slow_performance, 'System is running slowly').
symptom(strange_noise, 'Strange noise from computer').
symptom(no_internet, 'No internet connection').
symptom(overheating, 'Computer feels hot').
symptom(program_crash, 'Programs keep crashing').
symptom(disk_full, 'Hard drive full').

/* Rules for diagnosis */
diagnosis(Problem, Cause, Solution) :-
    problem(Problem, Cause),
    solution(Problem, Solution).

/* Problem causes */
problem(wont_boot, 'Power supply failure') :-
    verify(no_power_lights),
    verify(no_fan_noise).
```

```prolog
problem(wont_boot, 'RAM issue') :-
    verify(beeping_sound),
    verify(screen_remains_black).

problem(blue_screen, 'Driver conflict') :-
    verify(recent_hardware_change),
    verify(system_restarts).

problem(blue_screen, 'Hardware failure') :-
    verify(random_crashes),
    verify(system_unstable).

problem(slow_performance, 'Malware infection') :-
    verify(unexpected_popups),
    verify(high_cpu_usage).

problem(slow_performance, 'Low memory') :-
    verify(many_programs_running),
    verify(system_sluggish).

problem(strange_noise, 'Fan problem') :-
    verify(noise_from_fan_area),
    verify(temperature_increased).

problem(strange_noise, 'Hard drive failure') :-
    verify(clicking_sound),
    verify(slow_file_access).

/* Solutions */
solution(wont_boot, 'Replace power supply unit') :-
    problem(wont_boot, 'Power supply failure').

solution(wont_boot, 'Check and reseat RAM modules') :-
```

```
    problem(wont_boot, 'RAM issue').

solution(blue_screen, 'Roll back recent driver updates
    ') :-
    problem(blue_screen, 'Driver conflict').

solution(blue_screen, 'Run hardware diagnostics') :-
    problem(blue_screen, 'Hardware failure').

solution(slow_performance, 'Run antivirus scan') :-
    problem(slow_performance, 'Malware infection').

solution(slow_performance, 'Upgrade RAM or close
    programs') :-
    problem(slow_performance, 'Low memory').

/* User interface predicates */
:- dynamic(fact/1).

verify(Question) :-
    fact(Question), !.

verify(Question) :-
    \+ fact(Question),
    ask_question(Question, Answer),
    Answer = yes,
    assertz(fact(Question)).

ask_question(Question, Answer) :-
    format('~w? (yes/no): ', [Question]),
    read(Answer).

/* Clear facts between consultations */
```

```prolog
clear_facts :-
    retractall(fact(_)).

/* Main diagnostic procedure */
diagnose :-
    write('Computer Problem Diagnosis System'), nl,
    write('Please answer the following questions:'),
        nl,
    find_problem.

find_problem :-
    symptom(Problem, Description),
    write('Checking for: '), write(Description), nl,
    diagnosis(Problem, Cause, Solution),
    nl, write('Diagnosis complete:'), nl,
    write('Problem: '), write(Description), nl,
    write('Cause: '), write(Cause), nl,
    write('Recommended Solution: '), write(Solution),
        nl,
    clear_facts.

/* Example usage:
?- diagnose.
*/
```

Example 4: Natural Language Parser

Problem Description

Implement a simple natural language parser that can understand basic English sentences and generate their logical representation. This demonstrates Prolog's power in processing structured text and grammar rules.

Implementation

```
/* Simple Natural Language Parser */

/* Grammar Rules */
sentence(s(NP, VP)) -->
    noun_phrase(NP, Number),
    verb_phrase(VP, Number).

noun_phrase(np(Det, N), Number) -->
    determiner(Det, Number),
    noun(N, Number).

noun_phrase(np(PN), Number) -->
    proper_noun(PN, Number).

verb_phrase(vp(V, NP), Number) -->
    transitive_verb(V, Number),
    noun_phrase(NP, _).

verb_phrase(vp(V), Number) -->
    intransitive_verb(V, Number).
```

```
/* Lexicon */
determiner(det(the), _) --> [the].
determiner(det(a), singular) --> [a].
determiner(det(an), singular) --> [an].

noun(n(cat), singular) --> [cat].
noun(n(cats), plural) --> [cats].
noun(n(dog), singular) --> [dog].
noun(n(dogs), plural) --> [dogs].
noun(n(book), singular) --> [book].
noun(n(books), plural) --> [books].

proper_noun(pn(john), singular) --> [john].
proper_noun(pn(mary), singular) --> [mary].

transitive_verb(tv(sees), singular) --> [sees].
transitive_verb(tv(see), plural) --> [see].
transitive_verb(tv(likes), singular) --> [likes].
transitive_verb(tv(like), plural) --> [like].

intransitive_verb(iv(sleeps), singular) --> [sleeps].
intransitive_verb(iv(sleep), plural) --> [sleep].
intransitive_verb(iv(runs), singular) --> [runs].
intransitive_verb(iv(run), plural) --> [run].

/* Semantic Rules */
semantics(s(NP, VP), Meaning) :-
    np_semantics(NP, Subject),
    vp_semantics(VP, Subject, Meaning).

np_semantics(np(Det, N), Entity) :-
    det_semantics(Det, N, Entity).
np_semantics(np(PN), Entity) :-
```

```
    pn_semantics(PN, Entity).

vp_semantics(vp(V, NP), Subject, Meaning) :-
    tv_semantics(V, Relation),
    np_semantics(NP, Object),
    Meaning =.. [Relation, Subject, Object].
vp_semantics(vp(V), Subject, Meaning) :-
    iv_semantics(V, Relation),
    Meaning =.. [Relation, Subject].

/* Helper predicates for parsing */
parse(Sentence, Tree) :-
    phrase(sentence(Tree), Sentence).

parse_and_semantics(Sentence, Meaning) :-
    parse(Sentence, Tree),
    semantics(Tree, Meaning).

/* Pretty printing predicates */
print_tree(Tree) :-
    write_tree(Tree, 0).

write_tree(Term, Level) :-
    Term =.. [Functor|Args],
    tab(Level),
    write(Functor), nl,
    NextLevel is Level + 2,
    write_args(Args, NextLevel).

write_args([], _).
write_args([Arg|Args], Level) :-
    write_tree(Arg, Level),
    write_args(Args, Level).
```

```
/* Example usage:
?- parse([the, cat, sees, a, dog], Tree).
?- parse_and_semantics([john, likes, mary], Meaning).
?- parse([the, cats, sleep], Tree), print_tree(Tree).
*/

/* Test predicates */
test_parse(Sentence) :-
    parse(Sentence, Tree),
    write('Parse tree:'), nl,
    print_tree(Tree), nl,
    (parse_and_semantics(Sentence, Meaning) ->
        write('Semantic interpretation:'), nl,
        write(Meaning), nl
    ;
        write('No semantic interpretation available'),
            nl
    ).

test_all_parses(Sentence) :-
    findall(Tree, parse(Sentence, Tree), Trees),
    write('All possible parse trees:'), nl,
    print_trees(Trees).

print_trees([]).
print_trees([Tree|Trees]) :-
    print_tree(Tree), nl,
    print_trees(Trees).
```

Example 5: Constraint Logic Programming

Problem Description

Implement solutions to classic constraint satisfaction problems using Prolog's CLP(FD) library. This demonstrates Prolog's powerful constraint solving capabilities.

Implementation

```
/* Constraint Logic Programming Examples */
:- use_module(library(clpfd)).

/* 1. N-Queens Problem */
n_queens(N, Queens) :-
    length(Queens, N),
    Queens ins 1..N,
    safe_queens(Queens),
    labeling([], Queens).

safe_queens([]).
safe_queens([Q|Queens]) :-
    safe_queens(Queens, Q, 1),
    safe_queens(Queens).

safe_queens([], _, _).
safe_queens([Q|Queens], Q0, D0) :-
    Q0 #\= Q,
    abs(Q0 - Q) #\= D0,
    D1 #= D0 + 1,
    safe_queens(Queens, Q0, D1).
```

```
/* 2. Sudoku Solver */
sudoku(Rows) :-
    length(Rows, 9),
    maplist(same_length(Rows), Rows),
    append(Rows, Vs),
    Vs ins 1..9,
    maplist(all_distinct, Rows),
    transpose(Rows, Columns),
    maplist(all_distinct, Columns),
    Rows = [R1,R2,R3,R4,R5,R6,R7,R8,R9],
    blocks(R1,R2,R3), blocks(R4,R5,R6), blocks(R7,R8,
        R9),
    labeling([], Vs).

blocks([], [], []).
blocks([A,B,C|Bs1], [D,E,F|Bs2], [G,H,I|Bs3]) :-
    all_distinct([A,B,C,D,E,F,G,H,I]),
    blocks(Bs1, Bs2, Bs3).

/* 3. Map Coloring Problem */
map_coloring(Colors) :-
    Colors = [WA, NT, SA, Q, NSW, V, T],
    Colors ins 1..4,
    WA #\= NT, WA #\= SA,
    NT #\= SA, NT #\= Q,
    SA #\= Q, SA #\= NSW, SA #\= V,
    Q #\= NSW,
    NSW #\= V,
    labeling([], Colors).

/* 4. Scheduling Problem */
schedule_tasks(Tasks, MaxTime) :-
    Tasks = [Task1, Task2, Task3, Task4],
```

```
    Tasks ins 0..MaxTime,

    % Task durations
    Duration1 #= 2,
    Duration2 #= 3,
    Duration3 #= 4,
    Duration4 #= 2,

    % Ensure tasks complete within max time
    Task1 + Duration1 #=< MaxTime,
    Task2 + Duration2 #=< MaxTime,
    Task3 + Duration3 #=< MaxTime,
    Task4 + Duration4 #=< MaxTime,

    % Task dependencies
    Task2 #>= Task1 + Duration1,
    Task4 #>= Task2 + Duration2,
    Task4 #>= Task3 + Duration3,

    % Resource constraints
    nonoverlap([task(Task1,Duration1,1),
                task(Task2,Duration2,1),
                task(Task3,Duration3,1),
                task(Task4,Duration4,1)]),

    labeling([minimize(Task4)], Tasks).

/* 5. Knapsack Problem */
knapsack(Items, Capacity, Selection) :-
    length(Items, N),
    length(Selection, N),
    Selection ins 0..1,
```

```
% Calculate total weight and value
weights_values(Items, Weights, Values),
scalar_product(Weights, Selection, #=<, Capacity),
scalar_product(Values, Selection, #=, TotalValue),

labeling([maximize(TotalValue)], Selection).

weights_values([], [], []).
weights_values([(W,V)|Items], [W|Weights], [V|Values])
    :-
    weights_values(Items, Weights, Values).

/* Helper predicates */
print_solution(Name, Solution) :-
    write(Name), write(': '), write(Solution), nl.

print_sudoku([]).
print_sudoku([Row|Rows]) :-
    write(Row), nl,
    print_sudoku(Rows).

print_schedule(Tasks) :-
    Tasks = [T1,T2,T3,T4],
    write('Task 1 starts at: '), write(T1), nl,
    write('Task 2 starts at: '), write(T2), nl,
    write('Task 3 starts at: '), write(T3), nl,
    write('Task 4 starts at: '), write(T4), nl.

/* Example usage:
?- n_queens(8, Queens), print_solution('8-Queens',
   Queens
```

These examples demonstrate the power of Prolog's constraint

logic programming capabilities for solving complex problems. The code includes:

1. N-Queens Problem: Classical constraint satisfaction problem

2. Sudoku Solver: Grid-based constraint problem

3. Map Coloring Problem: Graph coloring with constraints

4. Scheduling Problem: Task scheduling with dependencies and resource constraints

5. Knapsack Problem: Optimization problem with constraints

Each problem showcases different aspects of constraint programming:

- Domain constraints ($ins/2$)

- Arithmetic constraints ($\# =, \# =, \# <, \# >$, etc.)

- Global constraints ($all\_distinct/1$, $nonoverlap/1$)

- Optimization ($minimize/1$, $maximize/1$)

- Labeling strategies

Answer Set Programming with Clingo

Example 1: Graph Coloring

Problem Description

Given an undirected graph, assign colors to vertices such that no
two adjacent vertices share the same color. The goal is to find
a valid coloring using the minimum number of colors possible.
The problem has applications in scheduling, register allocation,
and map coloring.

Implementation

```
% Define vertices and edges
vertex(1..6).
edge(1,2). edge(2,3). edge(3,4). edge(4,5). edge(5,6).
    edge(6,1).

% Available colors
color(red). color(blue). color(green).

% Each vertex must have exactly one color
1 { colored(V,C) : color(C) } 1 :- vertex(V).

% Adjacent vertices cannot have same color
:- edge(X,Y), colored(X,C), colored(Y,C).

% Make edges symmetric
edge(X,Y) :- edge(Y,X).
```

```
#show colored/2.
```

Example 2: Restaurant Menu Planning

Problem Description

Create a balanced restaurant menu that satisfies various dietary requirements and constraints. The menu must include items from different categories (appetizers, mains, desserts), ensure sufficient vegetarian and gluten-free options, and maintain variety in the selection.

Implementation

```
% Menu items and categories
dish(pasta_carbonara). dish(grilled_salmon).
dish(caesar_salad). dish(veggie_curry).
dish(chocolate_cake). dish(fruit_salad).

category(appetizer). category(main). category(dessert)
    .

% Properties of dishes
vegetarian(veggie_curry). vegetarian(caesar_salad).
contains_dairy(pasta_carbonara). contains_dairy(
    chocolate_cake).
gluten_free(grilled_salmon). gluten_free(fruit_salad).

% Assign dishes to categories
dish_category(caesar_salad, appetizer).
dish_category(pasta_carbonara, main).
dish_category(grilled_salmon, main).
dish_category(veggie_curry, main).
```

```
dish_category(chocolate_cake, dessert).
dish_category(fruit_salad, dessert).

% Select dishes for menu
{ selected(D) } :- dish(D).

% Menu constraints
:- category(C), not 1 { selected(D) : dish_category(D,
    C) }.
:- not 2 { selected(D) : vegetarian(D) }.
:- not 2 { selected(D) : gluten_free(D) }.

#show selected/1.
```

Example 3: Student Course Schedule

Problem Description

Generate a conflict-free course schedule for students, considering room availability, time slots, prerequisites, and credit load constraints. The schedule must ensure no student has overlapping classes and prerequisites are taken in the correct order.

Implementation

```
% Courses and time slots
course(math101). course(physics101). course(cs101).
course(english101). course(history101).

timeslot(1..5).
room(r1). room(r2). room(r3).

% Course requirements
credits(math101,3). credits(physics101,4).
credits(cs101,3). credits(english101,3).
credits(history101,3).

prerequisite(physics101, math101).

% Schedule generation
{ scheduled(C,T,R) : timeslot(T), room(R) } 1 :-
    course(C).

% Constraints
:- scheduled(C1,T,R), scheduled(C2,T,R), C1 != C2.
:- scheduled(C1,T,R1), scheduled(C2,T,R2), C1 != C2.
```

```
:- scheduled(C1,T1,_), scheduled(C2,T2,_),
   prerequisite(C1,C2), T1 <= T2.
:- timeslot(T),
   #sum { Cr,C : scheduled(C,T,_), credits(C,Cr) } >
      6.

#show scheduled/3.
```

Example 4: Map Territory Division

Problem Description

Divide a map into territories while maintaining contiguity and balanced population distribution. Each region must be assigned to exactly one territory, and territories should be connected. The solution must consider population balance and minimize border conflicts.

Implementation

```
% Regions and adjacency
region(1..10).
adjacent(1,2). adjacent(2,3). adjacent(3,4).
adjacent(4,5). adjacent(5,1). adjacent(2,6).
adjacent(3,7). adjacent(4,8). adjacent(5,9).

% Population data
population(1,1000). population(2,1500).
population(3,800). population(4,1200).
population(5,900). population(6,700).
population(7,1100). population(8,1300).
population(9,950). population(10,850).

% Territory assignment
territory(a). territory(b). territory(c).

% Assignment rules
1 { assigned(R,T) : territory(T) } 1 :- region(R).
```

```
% Connected territories constraint
connected(T) :- territory(T),
    #count { R : assigned(R,T) } > 0.

% Population balance
:- territory(T),
   #sum { P,R : assigned(R,T), population(R,P) } >
      4000.

% Territory cohesion
:- adjacent(R1,R2), assigned(R1,T1), assigned(R2,T2),
   T1 != T2, #count { R : assigned(R,T1) } < 3.

#show assigned/2.
```

Example 5: Social Network Analysis

Problem Description

Analyze a social network to detect communities, identify influential users, and make friend recommendations. The analysis considers user relationships, shared interests, and interaction patterns to create meaningful insights about the network structure.

Implementation

```
% Users and relationships
user(1..10).
follows(1,2). follows(2,3). follows(3,4).
follows(4,1). follows(5,1). follows(6,2).
follows(7,3). follows(8,4). follows(9,5).

% User interests
interest(gaming). interest(music). interest(sports).
interest(books). interest(movies).

has_interest(1,gaming). has_interest(1,music).
has_interest(2,sports). has_interest(2,gaming).
has_interest(3,books). has_interest(3,movies).
has_interest(4,music). has_interest(4,sports).

% Community detection
{ community(U,C) : C=1..3 } 1 :- user(U).

% Similar interests identification
similar_interests(U1,U2) :- user(U1), user(U2),
    has_interest(U1,I), has_interest(U2,I),
```

```
    U1 != U2.

% Calculate community cohesion
cohesion_score(S) :- S = #count {
    U1,U2 : similar_interests(U1,U2),
            community(U1,C), community(U2,C)
}.

% Calculate user influence
influence_score(U,S) :- user(U),
    S = #count { V : follows(V,U) }.

% Friend recommendations
potential_friend(U1,U2) :- user(U1), user(U2),
    similar_interests(U1,U2),
    not follows(U1,U2), not follows(U2,U1),
    U1 != U2.

#maximize { S : cohesion_score(S) }.
#show community/2.
#show potential_friend/2.
#show influence_score/2.
```